SIX SISTERS' STUFF

Healthy Eats

SIX SISTERS' STUFF

Healthy Eats

101+ DELICIOUS RECIPES AND TIPS FOR A HEALTHY FAMILY

SHADOW
MOUNTAIN

To moms,

trying in the chaos of their busy lives to

get something healthy on the table.

You got this!

Library of Congress Cataloging-in-Publication Data

Names: Six Sisters' Stuff, issuing body.
Title: Healthy eats with Six Sisters' Stuff : 101+ delicious recipes and tips for a healthy family / Six Sisters' Stuff.
Description: Salt Lake City, Utah : Shadow Mountain, [2020] | Includes index. | Summary: "Popular blogger Six Sisters' Stuff have gathered more than 100 of their most-requested healthy recipes that are not only quick-and-easy to make but also delicious"— Provided by publisher.
Identifiers: LCCN 2019041822 | ISBN 9781629727301 (paperback)
Subjects: LCSH: Quick and easy cooking. | LCGFT: Cookbooks.
Classification: LCC TX833.5 .H435 2020 | DDC 641.5/12—dc23
LC record available at https://lccn.loc.gov/2019041822

Printed in China
Four Colour Print Group, Nansha, China

10   9   8   7   6   5   4   3   2   1

contents

MAIN DISHES

SIDE DISHES

SNACKS AND DESSERTS

INTRODUCTION

If you haven't noticed by now, over at Six Sisters' Stuff we *love* food. We love that it brings people together, helps build lasting memories, and—of course—tastes *delicious*. We have been wanting to write a healthier cookbook for years, and when the opportunity arose, we jumped at the chance.

As a complete disclaimer, not one of us has a background in nutrition or dietetics. We've never studied food science or even attended culinary school! But we *do* know what it's like trying to find healthier recipes for dishes that taste good enough your family will eat them. We also realize that "healthy" is a completely subjective term and is different for everyone. For some, that may mean low-carb and high-fat; for others, it will be very little dairy and no gluten.

For us, we believe that all foods are best in moderation. When putting together this cookbook, we tried to keep the ingredients as minimally processed as possible, avoid pre-packaged foods and seasonings, and reduce sugars where we could.

You will find the nutritional information listed for each recipe in this book. Calculated by us, each recipe is under 500 calories. However, nutritional information can vary—even depending on the brand of a certain ingredient you use. The nutritional information should be considered more of a guideline to help you meet your personal nutritional goals.

So whether you're looking to lose weight, feed your family less-processed foods, or just maintain a more balanced lifestyle, we hope you find recipes here that your whole family will enjoy for breakfast, lunch, dinner, or dessert.

As always, thank you for purchasing our cookbooks and making our dreams a reality. None of this would be possible without all of you. From all six of us to you, *welcome to the sisterhood*.

—The Six Sisters

breakfast

HEARTY BREAKFAST COOKIES

Prep time: 15 minutes | Cook time: 15 minutes | Total time: 30 minutes | Yields: 12 cookies

1 medium ripe banana, mashed (yields about ½ cup)

¼ cup honey

¼ cup unsweetened applesauce

½ teaspoon ground cinnamon

1½ tablespoons chia seeds

2 cups quick oats

¾ cup peanut butter

¼ cup unsweetened shredded coconut

¼ cup cacao nibs

Preheat oven to 325 degrees F. Line a baking sheet with parchment paper.

In a large bowl, mix together mashed banana, honey, applesauce, cinnamon, and chia seeds. Stir in quick oats and peanut butter until combined well. Fold in coconut and cacao nibs.

Using a ⅓ cup measuring cup or a large cookie scoop, drop 12 scoops of dough onto prepared baking sheet. Flatten the cookies slightly with your hand, as they won't flatten on their own while they bake.

Bake 15 minutes, until cookies start to brown on the bottom and around the edges. Cool on wire racks before serving.

Per Serving (1 cookie): **Calories** 242 | **Fat** 14g | **Carb** 24.5g | **Fiber** 5g | **Sugar** 10.5g | **Protein** 7g

BLUEBERRY BREAKFAST COOKIES

Prep time: 15 minutes | Cook time: 20 minutes | Total time: 35 minutes | Yields: 18 cookies

- 2 medium ripe bananas, mashed (yields about 1 cup)
- 2½ cups old-fashioned rolled oats
- ½ cup any nut butter, such as almond or cashew butter
- ½ cup chopped pecans or walnuts

- ⅓ cup honey or agave
- 1 teaspoon vanilla extract
- ½ teaspoon ground cinnamon
- ¼ teaspoon salt
- 1 cup fresh or frozen blueberries (do not thaw frozen blueberries)

Preheat oven to 325 degrees F. Spray 2 baking sheets with nonstick cooking spray or line with parchment paper. Set aside.

In a large bowl, mix together mashed bananas, oats, nut butter, nuts, honey, vanilla, cinnamon, and salt until combined well. Gently fold in blueberries with a rubber spatula. Scoop 9 mounds of batter (about 3 tablespoons each) onto each baking sheet.

Bake 18 to 21 minutes, until lightly browned on the sides. Remove from oven and let cool on baking sheets 5 minutes before transferring to a wire rack to cool completely.

Cookies will stay fresh in an airtight container at room temperature for up to 1 week.

Per Serving (1 cookie): **Calories** 143 | **Fat** 7g | **Carb** 19g | **Fiber** 2.5g | **Sugar** 8g | **Protein** 3g

GREEK YOGURT BLUEBERRY MUFFINS

Prep time: 15 minutes | Cook time: 17 minutes | Total time: 32 minutes | Yields: 12 muffins

1 large egg

1 cup plain nonfat Greek yogurt

¼ cup skim milk

4 tablespoons coconut oil, melted

1 teaspoon vanilla extract

⅓ cup honey

¾ cup whole wheat flour

1 cup old-fashioned rolled oats

1 teaspoon baking powder

½ teaspoon baking soda

½ teaspoon ground cinnamon

¼ teaspoon ground nutmeg

¼ teaspoon salt

2 cups fresh blueberries, divided

Preheat oven to 375 degrees F. Line a standard muffin tin with 12 paper liners, or coat with nonstick cooking spray.

In a medium bowl, mix together the egg, yogurt, milk, coconut oil, vanilla, and honey. Set aside.

In a separate large mixing bowl combine the flour, oats, baking powder, baking soda, cinnamon, nutmeg, and salt.

Add the yogurt mixture to the dry ingredients and stir until just combined. Batter will still be a little lumpy.

Gently fold in 1½ cups of the blueberries with a rubber spatula. Divide batter evenly among prepared muffin cups. Top each muffin with a few of the remaining blueberries.

Bake 15 to 17 minutes, until muffin tops start turning golden brown and bounce back when touched lightly.

Let muffins rest in tin for a few minutes before removing and cooling on wire rack.

Per Serving (1 muffin): **Calories** 175 | **Fat** 5.5g | **Carb** 27.5g | **Fiber** 2.5g | **Sugar** 14g | **Protein** 5.5g

CHOCOLATE-BANANA BLENDER MUFFINS

Prep time: 10 minutes | Cook time: 15 minutes | Total time: 25 minutes | Yields: 12

2 large ripe bananas

2 large eggs

1 cup natural peanut butter, such as Smucker's Natural Creamy Peanut Butter

¾ cup old-fashioned rolled oats

½ cup honey

½ cup unsweetened cocoa powder

1 teaspoon baking powder

½ teaspoon salt

¼ cup water

Sugar-free mini chocolate chips, for sprinkling on top (optional)

Preheat oven to 350 degrees F. Line a standard muffin tin with 12 paper liners, or coat with nonstick cooking spray.

In a high-powered blender, add bananas, eggs, peanut butter, oats, honey, cocoa powder, baking powder, salt, and water. Blend until smooth and well mixed.

Scoop batter into prepared muffin tin, filling each cup about ¾ full. Sprinkle the top with chocolate chips, if desired.

Bake 13 to 15 minutes, or until a toothpick inserted in the center of a muffin comes out with just a few crumbs.

Remove from the oven and let cool for 5 minutes before removing from the pan to cool.

Per Serving (1 muffin): **Calories** 222 | **Fat** 12.5g | **Carb** 25.5g | **Fiber** 4g | **Sugar** 15g | **Protein** 8g

BANANA WALNUT MUFFINS

Prep time: 15 minutes | Cook time: 20 minutes | Total time: 35 minutes | Yields: 20 muffins

4 medium overripe bananas, mashed (yields about 2 cups)

1 large egg

⅓ cup nonfat plain Greek yogurt

2 tablespoons unsweetened applesauce

⅓ cup brown sugar

¼ cup pure maple syrup

1 teaspoon vanilla extract

1 teaspoon baking soda

½ teaspoon salt

1 teaspoon ground cinnamon

¼ teaspoon ground nutmeg

2 cups whole wheat flour

1 cup chopped walnuts

Preheat oven to 350 degrees F. Line 2 standard muffin tins with 20 paper liners, or coat with non-stick cooking spray.

In a large bowl, combine mashed banana, egg, Greek yogurt, applesauce, brown sugar, maple syrup, and vanilla until well combined.

Add baking soda, salt, cinnamon, nutmeg, and flour and mix until well combined. Fold in chopped walnuts.

Scoop batter into prepared muffin tins, filling each cup about ⅔ full.

Bake 20 to 22 minutes or until muffins are golden brown on top.

Per Serving (1 muffin): **Calories** 133 | **Fat** 4.5g | **Carb** 21.5g | **Fiber** 2.5g | **Sugar** 7g | **Protein** 3g

BAKED STRAWBERRY OATMEAL CUPS

Prep time: 10 minutes | Cook time: 20 minutes | Total time: 30 minutes | Serves: 14

4¼ cups old-fashioned rolled oats

1½ teaspoons ground cinnamon

1 teaspoon baking powder

½ teaspoon salt

½ cup vanilla protein powder

¼ cup coconut sugar or brown sugar

2½ cups skim milk or unsweetened almond milk

2 teaspoons vanilla extract

⅓ cup pure maple syrup

1 cup diced strawberries

Preheat oven to 375 degrees F. Line a standard muffin tin with 12 paper liners, or coat with nonstick cooking spray.

In a large bowl, combine oats, cinnamon, salt, baking powder, protein powder, and sugar. Stir in milk and maple syrup and combine well. Gently fold in strawberries with a rubber spatula.

Using a ¼ cup measure, scoop oatmeal mixture into prepared muffin tin, stirring between each scoop to recombine ingredients. (The milk and oats tend to separate if not remixed between scoops.)

Bake 20 minutes, or until edges begin to golden.

Cool muffins in tins for several minutes before moving to a wire rack to cool completely. Enjoy! Muffins can be frozen for several weeks. Simply place in resealable freezer bags, seal, and freeze. To serve: Thaw for 2 hours at room temperature or microwave on high for 10 seconds.

Per Serving (1 oatmeal cup): **Calories** 105 | **Fat** 1g | **Carb** 20g | **Fiber** 1.5g | **Sugar** 11g | **Protein** 4g

CINNAMON-BANANA BAKED OATMEAL

Prep time: 15 minutes | Cook time: 30 minutes | Total time: 45 minutes | Serves: 6

3 cups old-fashioned rolled oats

½ tablespoon ground cinnamon

1 teaspoon baking soda

½ teaspoon salt

½ cup chopped walnuts

3 medium ripe bananas, mashed

2 large eggs

¼ cup pure maple syrup

1 teaspoon vanilla extract

½ cup unsweetened almond milk

Preheat oven to 350 degrees F. Coat a 9x13-inch pan with nonstick cooking spray and set aside. In a large bowl, toss together oats, cinnamon, baking soda, salt, and walnuts until well combined. In a separate bowl, stir together mashed bananas, eggs, maple syrup, vanilla, and almond milk. Pour wet ingredients into the bowl of dry ingredients and stir to combine until all oats are coated. Pour oat mixture into prepared pan. If desired, top with additional chopped walnuts and sprinkle with cinnamon.

Bake 30 minutes and serve warm.

Per Serving: Calories 300 | **Fat** 11g | **Carb** 43g | **Fiber** 7g | **Sugar** 8g | **Protein** 10.5g

EASY PUMPKIN WAFFLES

Prep time: 15 minutes | Cook time: 6 minutes | Total time: 21 minutes | Yields: 10 large waffles

1 tablespoon unsalted butter, melted

1 cup pure pumpkin

6 large egg whites

2 tablespoons pure maple syrup

1 teaspoon vanilla extract

2¾ cups skim milk

2 teaspoons ground cinnamon

1 teaspoon ground allspice

½ teaspoon ground nutmeg

¼ teaspoon ground cloves

2 teaspoons baking powder

1 teaspoon baking soda

½ teaspoon salt

2½ cups whole wheat flour

Preheat waffle iron.

In a large bowl, whisk together melted butter and pumpkin puree. Add eggs whites, maple syrup, and vanilla and whisk again to combine well. Whisk in milk.

Add the spices, baking powder, baking soda, and salt and whisk until well combined.

Whisk in the whole wheat flour.

Cook waffles in greased, preheated waffle iron according to iron's directions.

To freeze waffles for up to 3 months, cool waffles completely, place in resealable plastic bags, seal tightly, and store in freezer. When ready to eat, thaw waffles and then gently warm or crisp them in a toaster or oven on low heat.

Per Serving (half of a large waffle): **Calories** 196 | **Fat** 6g | **Carb** 31g | **Fiber** 4g | **Sugar** 8g | **Protein** 8g

BLUEBERRY PROTEIN PANCAKES

Prep time: 10 minutes | Cook time: 5 minutes | Total time: 15 minutes | Yields: 12 pancakes

2 cups old-fashioned rolled oats

2 medium ripe bananas

4 large eggs

4 large egg whites

1 teaspoon baking soda

1⅓ cups vanilla protein powder

½ cup skim milk

1 cup blueberries

Pure maple syrup, for topping

Heat a nonstick griddle to medium-high heat, about 300 degrees F. on an electric griddle.

Add oats, bananas, eggs, egg whites, baking soda, protein powder, and milk to the jar of a blender and blend until smooth.

Add blueberries and pulse 2 to 3 times to blend in.

Spray griddle with nonstick cooking spray. Ladle ⅓ cup batter per pancake on griddle and cook until bubbles appear, about 1 to 2 minutes.

Flip pancakes and cook until golden brown, about 1 to 2 minutes. Remove from griddle and serve hot with pure maple syrup, if desired.

Per Serving (3 pancakes): **Calories** 323 | **Fat** 7g | **Carb** 38g | **Fiber** 4g | **Sugar** 5.5g | **Protein** 27.5g

BANANA-OAT PANCAKES

Prep time: 10 minutes | Cook time: 4 minutes | Total time: 14 minutes | Yields: 6 pancakes

2 medium ripe bananas, mashed

2 large eggs

⅓ cup skim milk

1 teaspoon vanilla extract

½ cup quick oats

⅓ cup whole wheat flour

1 teaspoon baking powder

½ teaspoon baking soda

1 teaspoon ground cinnamon

Heat nonstick griddle to 370 degrees F.

In a large bowl, stir together mashed bananas, eggs, milk, and vanilla until well combined.

Fold in oats, flour, baking powder, baking soda, and cinnamon.

Spray griddle lightly with nonstick cooking spray. Using a ⅓ cup measure, pour batter onto griddle. If needed, smooth out batter so it's evenly distributed. Cook until bubbles appear, about 1 to 2 minutes. Flip pancakes and cook until golden brown, about 1 to 2 minutes. Serve while hot.

Per Serving (1 pancake): **Calories** 116 | **Fat** 2g | **Carb** 20.5g | **Fiber** 2g | **Sugar** 6g | **Protein** 4.5g

SCRAMBLED-EGG BREAKFAST MUFFINS

Prep time: 20 minutes | Cook time: 20 minutes | Total time: 40 minutes | Yields: 12 muffins

2 teaspoons extra-virgin olive oil

3 tablespoons diced onion

¼ cup diced red bell pepper

¼ cup diced mushrooms

12 large eggs

½ teaspoon seasoned salt

Ground black pepper, to taste

¼ teaspoon garlic powder

1 cup diced cooked ham

1 cup reduced-fat shredded sharp cheddar cheese

½ cup finely chopped baby spinach

Preheat oven to 350 degrees F. Coat a standard muffin tin generously with nonstick cooking spray, or line the tin with heavy-duty (silicone) muffin liners.

Heat oil in a large skillet over medium-high heat until oil ripples; add onions, peppers, and mushrooms and sauté until tender, 8 to 10 minutes. Remove from heat and set aside.

In a large bowl, beat eggs until frothy. Whisk in seasoned salt, pepper, and garlic powder.

Fold in sautéed vegetables, ham, shredded cheese, and baby spinach.

Scoop ⅓ cup of the mixture into each muffin liner. Bake 20 to 25 minutes, until the center of the muffin is completely set.

Per Serving (1 muffin): **Calories** 122 | **Fat** 8.5g | **Carb** 1.5g | **Fiber** 0.3g | **Sugar** 0.5g | **Protein** 10g

LOADED BELL PEPPERS

Prep time: 8 minutes | Cook time: 6 minutes | Total time: 14 minutes | Serves: 4

4 large eggs

1 red bell pepper, sliced into 4¼- to ½-inch thick rings

½ cup roughly chopped spinach

2 tablespoons feta cheese crumbles

8 cherry tomatoes, sliced

Salt and pepper, to taste

Heat a nonstick skillet over medium heat. Layer pepper rings on the bottom of the hot skillet. Crack an egg into each pepper ring.

Sprinkle 2 tablespoons spinach, ½ tablespoon feta cheese crumbles, a few cherry tomato slices, and salt and pepper to taste over each egg.

For soft-cooked eggs, cook 3 to 5 minutes. For hard-cooked eggs, break up yolk slightly and cook 6 to 9 minutes.

Per Serving: Calories 130 | **Fat** 6g | **Carb** 12.5g | **Fiber** 3.5g | **Sugar** 8.5g | **Protein** 9g

BREAKFAST ENCHILADAS

Prep time: 20 minutes | Chilling and resting time: 90 minutes (or up to 10 hours) | Cook time: 35 minutes | Total time: 2 hours 25 minutes to 12 hours, depending on time in refrigerator | Serves: 8

---

1 cup diced fresh mushrooms

½ cup chopped green onions

1 red bell pepper, diced

1 green bell pepper, diced

2 cups chopped cooked chicken

8 (8-inch) whole wheat tortillas

1 cup skim milk

12 egg whites

¼ teaspoon salt

1 cup reduced-fat shredded cheddar cheese

Coat a 9x13-inch baking dish with nonstick cooking spray.

In a large skillet over medium-high heat, sauté mushrooms, green onions, red peppers, and green peppers until peppers are soft, about 8 to 10 minutes. Add chicken and stir until mixture is heated through.

Spoon ¼ cup of the chicken-and-vegetable mixture down the center of each tortilla.

Roll up tortillas and place seam side down in prepared baking dish.

In a large bowl, whisk together milk, eggs, and salt until combined well. Pour over tortillas.

Cover with aluminum foil and refrigerate at least 1 hour, or up to 10 hours.

30 minutes before baking, remove from the refrigerator and let the enchiladas rest on the counter-top. Preheat oven to 350 degrees F.

Bake, covered, 25 minutes. Remove aluminum foil, sprinkle with shredded cheese, and bake an additional 10 minutes.

Let stand for 10 minutes before serving.

Per Serving: Calories 284 | **Fat** 9g | **Carb** 27g | **Fiber** 4g | **Sugar** 4.5g | **Protein** 24g

RED-POTATO TURKEY-BACON BAKE

Prep time: 20 minutes | Cook time: 35 minutes | Total time: 55 minutes | Serves: 6

6 large red potatoes, washed and chopped into bite-sized pieces

2 tablespoons extra-virgin olive oil

½ small yellow onion, chopped

⅔ cup plain nonfat Greek yogurt

½ (1-ounce) packet ranch dressing mix

½ teaspoon ground black pepper

½ teaspoon garlic salt

8 strips turkey bacon, cooked and crumbled

½ cup reduced-fat shredded cheddar cheese

4 green onions, chopped

Preheat oven to 350 degrees F. Coat a 9x9-inch pan with nonstick cooking spray.

In a large bowl, toss the chopped red potatoes with olive oil and let potatoes rest 10 minutes.

Place oil-coated potatoes in prepared pan. Stir in chopped yellow onion and Greek yogurt.

Sprinkle potatoes with ranch dressing mix, pepper, and garlic salt; toss to coat with seasonings.

Cover the pan with aluminum foil and bake 15 minutes.

Remove from oven and sprinkle shredded cheese and crumbled bacon over top. Return to oven, uncovered, and bake an additional 15 to 20 minutes, or until the cheese is completely melted and the potatoes are tender and turning golden brown.

Garnish with chopped green onions before serving.

Per Serving: Calories 268 | **Fat** 9.5g | **Carb** 36g | **Fiber** 5.5g | **Sugar** 3g | **Protein** 11g

BREAKFAST TOSTADAS

Prep time: 15 minutes | Cook time: 5 minutes | Total time: 20 minutes | Serves: 4

4 tostada shells

1 red bell pepper, chopped

2 chicken sausage links, chopped

5 large eggs, beaten

½ cup chopped spinach

Salt and pepper, to taste

¼ cup reduced-fat shredded Mexican blend cheese

½ cup salsa (optional)

Preheat broiler to high. Place tostadas on a baking sheet and set aside.

In a large skillet over medium-high heat, cook peppers and chicken sausage until peppers are tender and sausage is heated through, about 10 minutes.

Add eggs, spinach, and salt and pepper and scramble until eggs are fully cooked, about 3 minutes.

Divide scrambled egg mixture evenly between the top of each tostada. Sprinkle 1 tablespoon shredded cheese on top of each tostada.

Broil 3 to 5 minutes, or until cheese is fully melted. If desired, serve topped with 2 tablespoons salsa. (Salsa is not included in nutrition information.)

Per Serving: Calories 304 | **Fat** 17g | **Carb** 22g | **Fiber** 1.5g | **Sugar** 2g | **Protein** 15g

BAGEL THIN EGG WHITE BREAKFAST SANDWICHES

Prep time: 10 minutes | Cook time: 20 minutes | Total time: 30 minutes | Serves: 4

8 egg whites

4 Thomas' Everything Bagel Thins Bagels, toasted

1 cup spinach

1 tomato, sliced

1 avocado, sliced

4 slices mozzarella cheese

4 tablespoons tomatillo salsa

Pour egg whites into a large nonstick skillet over medium heat. Let egg whites spread across bottom of the pan and cook until set, about 5 minutes. Slide egg whites off pan onto a clean plate and divide into 4 portions. (They should slide off all at once in a single piece, much like an omelet or fried egg.)

Top the bottom half of each toasted bagel thin with a portion of the egg whites, followed by equal portions of the spinach, tomato slices, avocado slices, mozzarella cheese, and tomatillo salsa. Top with remaining bagel thin halves.

Per Serving (1 sandwich): **Calories** 339 | **Fat** 13.5g | **Carb** 37.5g | **Fiber** 9g | **Sugar** 4g | **Protein** 23g

SWEET POTATO BREAKFAST BOWL

Prep time: 10 minutes | Cook time: 30 minutes | Total time: 40 minutes | Serves: 2

2 medium sweet potatoes, peeled and diced

2 tablespoons coconut oil, melted

1 teaspoon salt

2 tablespoons almond butter

2 tablespoons unsweetened coconut flakes

1 tablespoon chia seeds

1 tablespoon chopped pecans

½ cup blueberries

1 tablespoon raw honey

Preheat oven to 425 degrees F. Line a baking sheet with aluminum foil or coat with nonstick cooking spray.

Spread potatoes on prepared baking sheet and drizzle with coconut oil. Toss to coat potatoes in coconut oil.

Sprinkle with salt and bake 25 to 30 minutes, tossing every 10 minutes, until potatoes are tender and turning golden brown around the edges.

Transfer potatoes to 2 bowls and top each with 1 tablespoon almond butter, 1 tablespoon coconut flakes, ½ tablespoon chia seeds, ½ tablespoon chopped pecans, and ¼ cup blueberries. Drizzle with honey to taste.

Per Serving: Calories 393 | **Fat** 14.5g | **Carb** 62.5g | **Fiber** 11.5g | **Sugar** 14g | **Protein** 7.5g

ACAI SMOOTHIE BOWL

Prep time: 10 minutes | Freezing time: 2 hours minimum | Total time: 2 hours 10 minutes | Yields: 2 bowls

1 cup acai juice

¼ cup nonfat vanilla Greek yogurt

1 medium banana

4 whole strawberries

½ cup blueberries

½ cup raspberries

¼ cup granola

2 tablespoons unsweetened shredded coconut (optional)

At least 2 hours before preparing smoothie bowls, pour acai juice into ice cube trays and freeze. When ready to serve, blend together frozen acai juice, banana, yogurt, and strawberries. Pour smoothie into two bowls and top each with ¼ cup blueberries, ¼ cup raspberries, 2 tablespoons granola, and, if desired, 1 tablespoon coconut. We love drizzling a little honey or melted chocolate on top!

Per Serving (no toppings): **Calories** 119 | **Fat** 1.5g | **Carb** 25.5g | **Fiber** 2.3g | **Sugar** 16.5g | **Protein** 2.8g

IMMUNITY BOOSTING SMOOTHIE

Prep time: 5 minutes | Total time: 5 minutes | Yields: 2 smoothies

1 cup unsweetened almond milk

1 tablespoon freshly squeezed lemon juice

1 orange, peeled and cut

1 medium banana

1 cup frozen mango chunks

1 cup spinach

Add ingredients to blender in order listed and blend together until smooth. For a thicker consistency, add ice.

Per Serving: Calories 166 | **Fat** 2g | **Carb** 38g | **Fiber** 6g | **Sugar** 26.5g | **Protein** 2.5g

BANANA BREAKFAST SMOOTHIE

Prep time: 10 minutes | Total time: 10 minutes | Yields: 2 smoothies

1 cup unsweetened almond milk

2 medium frozen bananas

¼ cup creamy peanut butter

¼ cup old-fashioned rolled oats

2 teaspoons ground cinnamon

1 teaspoon vanilla extract

2 tablespoons unsweetened shredded coconut

Add ingredients to blender in order listed and blend well. Add additional almond milk as needed until desired consistency is reached.

Serve immediately.

Per Serving: Calories 422 | **Fat** 21g | **Carb** 52g | **Fiber** 9g | **Sugar** 18.5g | **Protein** 11.5g

lunch

BERRY ORANGE SPINACH SALAD

Prep time: 15 minutes | Total time: 15 minutes | Serves: 8

8 cups baby spinach, washed and rinsed

3 clementines, peeled and sectioned

¾ cup raspberries

¾ cup blackberries

¾ cup sliced strawberries

⅓ cup chopped walnuts

¼ cup feta cheese crumbles

1 recipe Citrus Dressing

In a large bowl, toss together spinach, clementine sections, and berries. Top with walnuts and feta cheese crumbles. Pour Citrus Dressing over top, toss lightly, and serve immediately. Alternatively, serve dressing separately from salad to reduce calorie, sugar, and fat.

Citrus Dressing

½ cup freshly squeezed orange juice

2 tablespoons olive oil

1½ tablespoons balsamic vinegar

¼ cup honey

In a medium bowl, whisk together orange juice, olive oil, balsamic vinegar, and honey until combined well.

Per Serving: Calories 157 | **Fat** 8g | **Carb** 20g | **Fiber** 3g | **Sugar** 15.5g | **Protein** 3.5g

BUFFALO-CHICKEN KALE SALAD

Prep time: 15 minutes | Total time: 15 minutes | Serves: 4

3 cups cooked, shredded chicken

¾ cup nonfat plain Greek yogurt

⅓ cup buffalo wing sauce

Salt and pepper, to taste

4 cups kale, rinsed and patted dry

½ cup chopped cucumber

⅓ cup shredded Parmesan cheese

⅓ cup low-fat ranch dressing

In a medium bowl, combine shredded chicken, Greek yogurt, and buffalo wing sauce until well combined. Season with salt and pepper to taste.

In a large bowl, toss kale with chicken mixture, cucumbers, Parmesan cheese, and ranch dressing. Alternatively, layer the ingredients, beginning with the kale and followed by chicken mixture, cucumbers, Parmesan cheese, and dressing.

Serve immediately or refrigerate in airtight container up to 3 days.

Per Serving: Calories 336 | **Fat** 10.5g | **Carb** 169mg | **Fiber** 0.5g | **Sugar** 2g | **Protein** 56g

HEALTHY AVOCADO CHICKEN SALAD

Prep time: 15 minutes | Total time: 15 minutes | Serves: 4

4 cups cooked, shredded chicken

2 avocados, diced

1 cucumber, diced

⅓ cup diced red onion

2 tablespoons freshly chopped cilantro

1 cup halved cherry tomatoes

1 recipe Lime Dressing

In a large bowl, toss together shredded chicken, avocados, cucumbers, red onions, cilantro, and cherry tomatoes.

Pour Lime Dressing over the chicken and veggies and toss until well combined. Serve immediately.

Lime Dressing

4 tablespoons freshly squeezed lime juice

2 tablespoons olive oil

¼ teaspoon garlic salt

½ teaspoon ground black pepper

½ teaspoon crushed red pepper flakes

In a small bowl, whisk together lime juice, olive oil, garlic salt, pepper, and crushed red pepper flakes. Use immediately or store in an airtight container up to 1 week. Shake well before using.

Per Serving: Calories 323 | **Fat** 21g | **Carb** 15g | **Fiber** 6.5g | **Sugar** 3.5g | **Protein** 24.5g

GRILLED SALMON SALAD

Prep time: 40 minutes | Cook time: 20 minutes | Total time: 1 hour | Serves: 4

---

4 (4-ounce) salmon fillets

1½ tablespoons coconut sugar

1 (20-ounce) can pineapple slices, juice reserved

2 tablespoons lower-sodium soy sauce

½ teaspoon dry mustard

2 teaspoons minced garlic

½ teaspoon red pepper flakes

2 tablespoons vinegar

2 tablespoons olive oil

4 cups baby spinach leaves

24 cherry tomatoes

1 avocado, sliced

⅓ cup feta cheese crumbles

Lay salmon fillets in a 9x9-inch baking dish or large shallow bowl and set aside.

In a small bowl, make a marinade by combining coconut sugar, ½ cup reserved juice from pineapple slices, soy sauce, mustard, garlic, and red pepper flakes.

Pour half of the marinade over the salmon. Cover remaining marinade and refrigerate for later use. Marinate salmon in refrigerator for 15 minutes. Turn over fillets and marinate another 10 minutes.

While fillets are marinating, preheat oven to 400 degrees F. Line a rimmed baking sheet with aluminum foil and coat lightly with nonstick cooking spray.

Place salmon, skin side down, on prepared baking sheet and bake 15 to 20 minutes, or until salmon flakes easily with a fork.

While the salmon is cooking, heat a grill pan to medium and grill the pineapple sliced 1 to 2 minutes on each side.

Remove reserved marinade from refrigerator, uncover, and whisk in vinegar and olive oil to make a salad dressing.

Divide spinach leaves between 4 salad plates. Arrange equal portions of the grilled pineapple slices, tomatoes, avocados, and cheese crumbles on each plate. Top each plate with a cooked salmon fillet. Drizzle salad dressing over top and serve.

Per Serving: Calories 469 | **Fat** 24g | **Carb** 35g | **Fiber** 5.5g | **Sugar** 27.5g | **Protein** 32g

AVOCADO-TUNA LETTUCE WRAPS

Prep time: 10 minutes | Total time: 10 minutes | Serves: 4

2 (4-ounce) cans tuna

2 avocados, chopped

1 red bell pepper, chopped

½ tablespoon freshly chopped dill

8 romaine lettuce leaves, washed and dried

Salt and pepper, to taste

½ tablespoon freshly squeezed lemon juice

1 bunch sprouts (optional)

Drain tuna and remove from can.

In a small bowl, toss together tuna, avocado, red pepper, and dill.

Fold in lemon juice and season with salt and pepper to taste.

Divide salad onto four lettuce leaves and top with sprouts if desired.

Per Serving: Calories 323 | **Fat** 24.5g | **Carb** 11.5g | **Fiber** 7.5g | **Sugar** 2g | **Protein** 17.5g

FLATBREAD VEGGIE PIZZA

Prep time: 10 minutes | Cook time: 10 minutes | Total time: 20 minutes | Serves: 3

3 flatbreads, such as Flatout Rustic White Artisan Thin Pizza Crusts

½ cup pizza sauce

1 cup shredded 2% milk mozzarella cheese

1 medium zucchini, thinly sliced

¼ cup diced onion

3 canned artichoke hearts, diced

¾ cup spinach

1 cup diced tomatoes

Preheat oven to 350 degrees F.

Place flatbreads on a baking sheet. Spread pizza sauce on each flat bread, and then top with cheese, vegetables, and diced tomatoes.

Bake 10 minutes, until cheese is melted and bubbly.

Per Serving (1 flatbread): **Calories** 323.5 | **Fat** 9g | **Carb** 41.5g | **Fiber** 7.5g | **Sugar** 9g | **Protein** 21.5g

GREEK VEGETABLE PITAS

Prep time: 10 minutes | Total time: 10 minutes | Serves: 4

½ cup diced red onion

1 cup chopped cherry tomatoes

1 tablespoon olive oil

1 tablespoon red wine vinegar or balsamic vinegar

1 teaspoon dried oregano

Salt and pepper, to taste

¼ cup hummus

1 small cucumber, diced

1 cup spinach

4 whole wheat pitas

⅔ cup feta cheese crumbles

Sprouts (optional)

In a small bowl, toss together onions and tomatoes. Add olive oil, vinegar, oregano, and salt and pepper to taste. Toss to coat.

Spread 1 tablespoon hummus on the bottom of each pita. Divide cucumbers and spinach evenly between each pita, layering the veggies over the hummus.

Top each pita with tomato and onion mixture, followed by cheese crumbles. If desired, top with sprouts.

Per Serving: Calories 343 | **Fat** 13g | **Carb** 46g | **Fiber** 8g | **Sugar** 2.5g | **Protein** 14g

EASY VEGETABLE WRAPS

Prep time: 20 minutes | Total time: 20 minutes | Serves: 2

½ cup 2% milkfat cottage cheese

4 teaspoons Dijon mustard

2 (8-inch) whole wheat wraps or tortillas

1 cup baby spinach

2 small carrots, peeled and grated

¼ cup diced red bell pepper

2 tablespoons diced red onion

1 tablespoon unsalted sunflower seeds

Salt and pepper, to taste

In a small bowl, stir together cottage cheese and Dijon mustard. Spread half of the cottage cheese mixture over each tortilla or wrap, stopping about 1 centimeter from the edges. Layer ½ cup spinach leaves over cottage cheese mixture on each tortilla. Arrange half of the carrots, bell peppers, and onions in a wide line down the middle of each tortilla. Sprinkle half of the sunflower seeds on top of each line of veggies.

Season with salt and pepper to taste. Fold in an inch of the tortilla on each side and then roll up tortilla from the bottom.

Cut each wrap in half and serve.

Per Serving: Calories 263 | **Fat** 7g | **Carb** 38g | **Fiber** 7g | **Sugar** 7g | **Protein** 13.5g

SKINNY CHICKEN SALAD SANDWICHES

Prep time: 10 minutes | Total time: 10 minutes | Serves: 4

2 cups cooked, shredded chicken

½ cup diced celery

½ cup halved red grapes

¼ cup dried cranberries

¼ cup chopped pecans

1 cup plain nonfat Greek yogurt

1 tablespoon freshly squeezed lemon juice

½ teaspoon garlic powder

Salt and pepper, to taste

4 whole wheat sandwich thins, such as Arnold 100% Whole Wheat Sandwich Thins

In a large mixing bowl, combine chicken, celery, grapes, cranberries, and pecans.

Fold in Greek yogurt and lemon juice.

Add garlic powder and salt and pepper to taste. Mix until well combined.

Spread chicken salad onto sandwich thins.

Per Serving (1 sandwich): **Calories** 379.5 | **Fat** 9.6g | **Carb** 39g | **Fiber** 6.5g | **Sugar** 15.5g | **Protein** 37.5g

PROTEIN-PACKED EGG SALAD SANDWICHES

Prep time: 20 minutes | Total time: 20 minutes | Serves: 4

4 hard-boiled eggs, peeled and diced

¾ cup fat-free cottage cheese

1 tablespoon yellow mustard

⅓ cup diced dill pickles

¼ teaspoon dried dill

½ teaspoon lemon juice

Salt and pepper, to taste

4 whole wheat sandwich thins, such as Arnold 100% Whole Wheat Sandwich Thins

In a large mixing bowl, mix together eggs, cottage cheese, mustard, pickles, dill, lemon juice, and salt and pepper until well combined.

Serve on sandwich thins.

Per Serving: Calories 159 | **Fat** 5.5g | **Carb** 14.5g | **Fiber** 1.5g | **Sugar** 8g | **Protein** 13.5g

AVOCADO BLACK BEAN QUESADILLAS

Prep time: 5 minutes | Cook time: 20 minutes | Total time: 25 minutes | Serves: 4

1 tablespoon olive oil

1 small onion, sliced

1 green bell pepper, sliced

½ cup black beans, drained and rinsed

1 tablespoon lower-sodium taco seasoning

2 avocados

¼ cup freshly minced cilantro

1 tablespoon freshly squeezed lime juice

Salt and pepper, to taste

4 (8-inch) whole wheat tortillas

1 cup shredded 2% milk mozzarella cheese

Heat oil in a large nonstick skillet over medium-high heat until oil ripples. Sauté onion and bell pepper 3 to 4 minutes, or until just becoming tender. Stir in black beans and taco seasoning and cook to warm through, about 1 minute. Transfer mixture to a small bowl and set aside.

In a small bowl, lightly mash the avocado with a fork. Stir in cilantro and lime juice; season with salt and pepper to taste. Spread a quarter of mashed avocado mixture onto half of a tortilla. Top with ¼ of the bean mixture and ¼ cup of cheese. Fold the tortilla closed over the veggies. Repeat until all tortillas are filled and all fillings are used.

Cook in large, nonstick skillet over medium-high heat for 2 to 3 minutes per side, or until the outside is crispy and cheese has fully melted.

Per Serving: Calories 438 | Fat 25g | Carb 42g | Fiber 12g | Sugar 4.5g | Protein 15g

BUFFALO CHICKEN TOSTADAS

Prep Time: 10 mins | Cook Time: 3 mins | Total Time: 13 mins | Serves: 6

---

5 to 6 chicken breasts, boneless and skinless, cooked and shredded

½ cup buffalo sauce

1½ cups plain Greek yogurt

10 to 12 tostada rounds

3 cups mozzarella cheese

¼ cup green onion

Cilantro, for garnish

Place the shredded chicken in a large bowl.

In a separate medium-sized bowl, combine the buffalo sauce and plain Greek yogurt, until fully combined. Add sauce to the shredded chicken. Fold until fully combined.

Place the tostada shells on a cookie sheet. Spread ½ cup of the chicken mixture over each shell. Sprinkle ⅓ cup of mozzarella cheese over the chicken.

Broil tostadas for about 3 minutes or until cheese is melted and chicken is warm.

Garnish with green onions and cilantro, if desired.

Per Serving: Calories 350 | **Fat** 7.2g | **Carbs** 15.4g | **Fiber** 4g | **Sugar** 4g | **Protein** 40g

MAKE-AHEAD RICE AND BEAN BURRITOS

Prep time: 15 minutes | Cook time: 15 minutes | Total time: 30 minutes | Serves: 6

2 tablespoons olive oil, divided

1 green bell pepper, sliced thin

1 red bell pepper, sliced thin

½ small onion, sliced thin

3 cups fat-free refried beans

6 (8-inch) whole wheat tortillas

1 cup cooked brown rice

½ cup salsa

½ cup reduced-fat shredded cheddar cheese

Preheat oven to 375 degrees F. Line a baking sheet with aluminum foil.

Heat 1 tablespoon olive oil in a large skillet over medium-high heat until oil ripples but doesn't smoke. Add peppers and onions and sauté until browned and soft, about 10 minutes.

While the peppers and onions are cooking, heat refried beans in a microwave-safe bowl for 30 seconds so they are easier to spread.

Top each tortilla with an equal portion of beans, rice, peppers, onions, salsa, and shredded cheese.

Tuck in the sides of each tortilla, then roll up from the bottom and place seam-side down on prepared baking sheet. Brush the tops with remaining olive oil, and then bake 15 minutes, until tops start to turn light golden brown.

Let burritos cool completely and then wrap in foil and place in a freezer-safe container. Freeze up to 30 days. When ready to serve, unwrap burrito and reheat in microwave 1 to 2 minutes on high power.

Per Serving (1 burrito): **Calories** 351 | **Fat** 10g | **Carb** 51g | **Fiber** 9.5g | **Sugar** 4.5g | **Protein** 14g

SHREDDED BEEF AND SWEET POTATO TACOS

Prep time: 20 minutes | Cook time: 6 hours 15 minutes | Total time: 6 hours 35 minutes | Serves: 6

1 (1.5- to 2-pound) boneless chuck roast

1 (14.5-ounce) can lower-sodium beef broth

2 medium sweet potatoes, peeled and cubed

1 small onion, diced

1 (1-ounce) packet lower-sodium taco season-ing, divided

½ cup water

2 tablespoons olive oil

⅓ cup light sour cream

2 teaspoons hot sauce

2 tablespoons freshly chopped cilantro

6 (8-inch) flour tortillas

Place roast in slow cooker. Pour beef broth over top, cover, and cook on low 6 hours.

During the last 30 minutes of cooking time, prepare the sweet potatoes. Layer potatoes in the bottom of a large skillet. Sprinkle with diced onions and all but ½ teaspoon of the taco seasoning. Pour water over all, cover, and cook 10 minutes over medium heat, until water has nearly evaporated and potatoes are almost tender.

Toss potato mixture with olive oil and cook 2 to 3 minutes, until potatoes are fork tender and starting to brown.

In a small bowl, stir together sour cream, hot sauce, and remaining ½ teaspoon taco seasoning until smooth and creamy; set aside for dipping.

When beef is done cooking, shred with a fork and stir into potato mixture.

Spoon mixture onto tortillas and garnish with chopped cilantro. Serve with dipping sauce.

Per Serving: Calories 434 | **Fat** 30g | **Carb** 9.5g | **Fiber** 1g | **Sugar** 3g | **Protein** 29g

SWEET POTATO TACO BOWLS

Prep time: 10 minutes | Cook time: 25 minutes | Total time: 35 minutes | Serves: 4

1 tablespoon chili powder

¼ teaspoon garlic powder

¼ teaspoon onion powder

¼ teaspoon dried oregano

½ teaspoon paprika

1½ teaspoons ground cumin

1 teaspoon salt

1 teaspoon ground black pepper

4 cups peeled and cubed sweet potatoes

1 tablespoon olive oil

2 cups canned black beans, drained and rinsed

1 cup corn

2 cups shredded lettuce

1 cup sliced cherry tomatoes

1 avocado, sliced

Freshly chopped cilantro, for topping

Salsa (optional)

Salad dressing (optional)

Preheat oven to 400 degrees F. Line a rimmed baking sheet with aluminum foil.

In a small bowl, mix together chili powder, garlic powder, onion powder, oregano, paprika, cumin, and salt and pepper.

With your hands, toss sweet potatoes with olive oil and the seasonings on prepared baking sheet. Bake 15 minutes, then remove from the oven and toss potatoes. Return to oven and bake another 10 to 15 minutes, until sweet potatoes are tender.

When the potatoes are finished cooking, divide evenly between 4 bowls. Top each bowl with an equal portion of beans, corn, lettuce, tomatoes, avocado, and cilantro. If desired, top with your favorite salsa or salad dressing. (Salsa or salad dressing are not included in nutrition information.)

Per Serving: Calories 422 | **Fat** 15g | **Carb** 67.5g | **Fiber** 16g | **Sugar** 4.5g | **Protein** 9g

MEDITERRANEAN BOWLS

Prep time: 10 minutes | Total time: 10 minutes | Serves: 4

1 cup quinoa, such as Bob's Red Mill Whole Grain Quinoa

2 medium cucumbers, chopped

1 (15-ounce) can chickpeas, drained and rinsed

½ cup prepared hummus

½ cup kalamata olives

½ cup chopped red onion

½ cup feta cheese crumbles

4 teaspoons olive oil

4 teaspoons balsamic vinegar

Chopped parsley (optional)

Cook quinoa according to package directions.

In four separate bowls, evenly layer quinoa, cucumbers, chickpeas, hummus, olives, red onions, and feta cheese.

Drizzle 1 teaspoon olive oil and 1 teaspoon balsamic vinegar over the top of each bowl. If desired, garnish with chopped parsley.

Per Serving: Calories 343 | **Fat** 14.5g | **Carb** 43.5g | **Fiber** 8.5g | **Sugar** 4g | **Protein** 13g

BUFFALO-CHICKEN SWEET POTATOES

Prep time: 10 minutes | Cook time: 30 minutes | Total time: 40 minutes | Serves: 4

4 sweet potatoes, scrubbed

2 cups cooked, shredded chicken

½ cup Frank's RedHot Original Cayenne Pepper Sauce

¼ cup ranch dressing

Salt and pepper, to taste

Preheat oven to 400 degrees F.

Pierce sweet potatoes with a fork and place on baking sheet. Bake 30 minutes, or until flesh is tender when pierced with a fork.

When sweet potatoes are tender, remove from oven and cool slightly, until they are easier to handle. Carefully cut sweet potatoes in half, leaving the skins connected.

Top each potato with ½ cup shredded chicken, 2 tablespoons Frank's sauce and 1 tablespoon ranch dressing. Add salt and pepper to taste.

Per Serving: **Calories** 372 | **Fat** 17g | **Carb** 29g | **Fiber** 4g | **Sugar** 6g | **Protein** 25g

CAJUN CHICKEN-SAUSAGE BAKE

Prep time: 15 minutes | Cook time: 30 minutes | Total time: 45 minutes | Serves: 4

1 medium sweet potato, diced

½ cup diced carrots

1 tablespoon olive oil

4 chicken sausage links, sliced

1 cup sliced mushrooms

⅓ small red onion, cut into pieces

¼ teaspoon Cajun seasoning

½ teaspoon ground black pepper

½ teaspoon garlic salt

¼ teaspoon onion powder

Preheat oven to 350 degrees F.

On a large, rimmed baking sheet, toss sweet potatoes and carrots with olive oil to coat.

Bake 20 to 25 minutes, until the sweet potatoes are tender when pierced with a fork.

Meanwhile, in a large nonstick skillet, sauté chicken sausage, mushrooms, and red onions over medium heat.

In a small bowl, combine Cajun seasoning, pepper, garlic salt, and onion salt; sprinkle over sausage and veggies as they cook. When sausage is cooked through and turning golden brown, add sweet potatoes and carrots and stir to combine. Cook until flavors are blended, about 5 minutes. Serve warm.

Per Serving: Calories 225 | **Fat** 12.5g | **Carb** 14.5g | **Fiber** 2.5g | **Sugar** 3.5g | **Protein** 16g

main dishes

GRILLED CAJUN-LIME CHICKEN

Prep time: 1 hour 10 minutes | Cook time: 16 minutes | Total time: 1 hour 26 minutes | Serves: 5

2 tablespoons olive oil

¼ teaspoon garlic salt

½ teaspoon ground black pepper

½ teaspoon Cajun seasoning

4 tablespoons freshly squeezed lime juice

¼ cup Worcestershire sauce

¼ teaspoon ground cumin

5 (4-ounce) boneless skinless chicken breasts

2 limes, sliced

In a large, resealable plastic bag, combine olive oil, garlic salt, pepper, Cajun seasoning, lime juice, Worcestershire sauce, and cumin. Add chicken breasts and seal bag. Massage and rotate the chicken breasts until coated. Marinade in refrigerator 1 hour, or overnight.

When ready to serve, heat grill pan to medium. Remove breasts from marinade and shake slightly to remove excess marinade. Grill 6 to 8 minutes on each side, or until chicken is cooked through and juices run clear.

Top each breast with 1 or 2 lime slices and serve.

Per Serving: Calories 226 | **Fat** 3.9g | **Carb** 5.7g | **Fiber** 0.2g | **Sugar** 3g | **Protein** 41.8g

HONEY-LIME GRILLED CHICKEN

Prep time: 10 minutes plus marinade time | Cook time: 15 minutes | Total time: 25 minutes | Serves: 4

½ cup freshly squeezed lime juice

⅓ cup vegetable oil

3 tablespoons honey

1 teaspoon dried thyme

1 teaspoon dried rosemary

3 cloves garlic, minced

½ teaspoon ground black pepper

4 (4-ounce) boneless skinless chicken breasts

In a large, resealable plastic bag, combine lime juice, oil, honey, thyme, rosemary, garlic, and pepper.

Place chicken breasts in bag, seal bag, and shake bag to coat chicken with marinade. Refrigerate at least 3 hours or overnight.

When ready to prepare chicken, preheat grill to high.

Remove breasts from bag and discard marinade. Grill 5 to 7 minutes on each side, until juices run clear and temperature registers 160 degrees F. on an instant-read thermometer inserted in the thickest part of the breast.

Per Serving: **Calories** 274 | **Fat** 9g | **Carb** 16.5g | **Fiber** 0.5g | **Sugar** 13.4g | **Protein** 33g

CHICKEN CORDON BLEU

Prep time: 15 minutes | Cook time: 30 minutes | Total time: 45 minutes | Serves: 6

6 (4-ounce) boneless skinless chicken breasts

¼ teaspoon salt

¼ teaspoon ground pepper

6 slices deli ham

¾ cup shredded Asiago cheese

⅓ cup Italian bread crumbs

Preheat oven to 350 degrees F. Coat a 9x13-inch baking dish with nonstick cooking spray.

Lay chicken breasts out on a piece of plastic wrap. Cover with another piece of plastic wrap and then use a meat mallet or rolling pin to pound chicken to about a ¼-inch thickness.

Sprinkle chicken breasts with salt and pepper. Top each breast with a slice of ham and 2 tablespoons shredded cheese.

Roll up each breast, tuck in ends, and secure with toothpicks.

Transfer to prepared dish. Sprinkle bread crumbs lightly over each chicken bundle. Bake 30 to 40 minutes, until juices run clear.

Per Serving: Calories 291 | **Fat** 10g | **Carb** 6.5g | **Fiber** 0g | **Sugar** 1g | **Protein** 41g

SPINACH- AND CHEESE-STUFFED CHICKEN BUNDLES

Prep time: 20 minutes | Cook time: 40 minutes | Total time: 1 hour | Serves: 8

---

4 ounces reduced-fat Neufchatel cheese, softened

1 (10-ounce) package frozen chopped spinach, thawed and drained

1½ cups shredded 2% milk mozzarella cheese, divided

¼ cup shredded Parmesan cheese

Salt and pepper, to taste

4 (4-ounce) boneless skinless chicken breasts

2 large eggs

1 cup whole wheat panko breadcrumbs

1 cup marinara sauce

Preheat oven to 375 degrees F. Coat a 9x13-inch baking dish with nonstick cooking spray.

In a medium mixing bowl, combine softened cream cheese, drained spinach, 1 cup of the shredded mozzarella, and the grated Parmesan cheese.

Season with salt and pepper to taste.

Prepare chicken breasts by slicing each breast in half widthwise to make two ¼-inch thick pieces. Place a few tablespoons of spinach mixture on the widest end of each chicken breast.

Roll up each breast and secure with a toothpick; set aside.

Whisk eggs in a shallow bowl and set aside. Place breadcrumbs in a separate shallow bowl.

Dip each chicken bundle in egg until coated, then roll in bread crumbs and place bundle in prepared baking dish.

Bake 30 minutes.

Remove from oven, carefully remove all toothpicks, and spoon 2 tablespoons of marinara sauce on top of each chicken bundle. Top with a sprinkle of the remaining mozzarella cheese.

Return to the oven and bake an additional 10 minutes.

Per Serving: Calories 281.5 | **Fat** 12g | **Carb** 12.5g | **Fiber** 2.5g | **Sugar** 2.5g | **Protein** 30g

EASY CHICKEN STREET TACOS

Prep time: 15 minutes | Cook time: 8 minutes | Total time: 23 minutes | Serves: 6

---

1 tablespoon olive oil

3 cups cooked and shredded chicken

1 teaspoon ground cumin

1½ teaspoons chili powder

1 teaspoon garlic powder

½ teaspoon salt

½ teaspoon ground black pepper

½ small onion, diced

2 Roma tomatoes, diced

½ cup freshly chopped cilantro

12 (6-inch) corn tortillas

¼ cup feta cheese crumbles

2 limes, cut into wedges

In a skillet over medium heat, combine olive oil, shredded chicken, cumin, chili powder, garlic powder, salt, and pepper and cook until completely heated through.

In a small bowl, gently toss together chopped onion, diced tomatoes, and cilantro.

To assemble tacos, lay a corn tortilla out flat on a plate.

Top with ¼ cup shredded chicken, a spoonful tomato mixture, and a few feta cheese crumbles. Squeeze the juice of a lime wedge over taco and serve.

Per Serving (2 tacos): **Calories** 371 | **Fat** 13.5g | **Carb** 25.5g | **Fiber** 2.5g | **Sugar** 2g | **Protein** 37.5g

CHICKEN PESTO AND ASPARAGUS SKILLET

Prep time: 10 minutes | Cook time: 25 minutes | Total time: 35 minutes | Serves: 6

---

3 tablespoons olive oil

1½ pounds boneless, skinless chicken tenderloins, sliced into strips

Salt and pepper, to taste

½ cup drained and chopped sun-dried tomatoes

1 pound asparagus, ends trimmed and cut in half

1 cup broccoli florets

½ cup basil pesto (see note)

1½ cups halved cherry tomatoes

Note: You can prepare your own pesto, but a jarred variety—such as Kirkland Signature Basil Pesto or Biutoni Pesto with Basil—works just as well. This recipe was tested using Kirkland Signature Basil Pesto.

Heat olive oil in a large skillet over medium heat. Season chicken tenders with salt and pepper then add to skillet along with sun-dried tomatoes. Sauté 7 to 10 minutes, until chicken is cooked through. Remove chicken and tomatoes from skillet and set aside.

Add asparagus and broccoli to hot skillet and sauté 6 to 10 minutes, until crisp tender. Remove vegetables from skillet.

Return chicken and tomatoes to skillet and stir in pesto. Cook over medium heat until chicken is heated through. Stir in cherry tomatoes and cooked vegetables.

Remove from heat and serve warm.

Per Serving: Calories 309 | **Fat** 17.5g | **Carb** 11g | **Fiber** 4.5g | **Sugar** 4g | **Protein** 27g

BARBECUE CHICKEN AND ROASTED SWEET POTATO BOWLS

Prep time: 10 minutes | Cook time: 35 minutes | Total time: 45 minutes | Serves: 4

---

3 medium sweet potatoes, peeled and diced

1 large yellow onion, chopped into 1-inch pieces

2 tablespoons olive oil, divided

¾ teaspoon salt, divided

¾ teaspoon garlic powder

¾ teaspoon chipotle powder or chili powder

4 cups broccoli florets

4 boneless skinless chicken breasts (see note)

¾ cup barbecue sauce, divided

Note: Use chicken breasts that are average in size for this recipe. Extra-large or extra-thick chicken breasts will take longer than 15 to 20 minutes to cook, which may cause the broccoli to turn mushy. Look for breasts that are about 4 ounces each.

Preheat the oven to 400 degrees F. Line a rimmed baking sheet with aluminum foil.

On prepared pan, toss sweet potatoes and onions with 1 tablespoon of the olive oil, ½ teaspoon of the salt, the garlic powder, and the chipotle powder until well combined. Bake 20 minutes.

Flip over the sweet potatoes and push them to one side of the pan. Add the broccoli florets and toss with remaining 1 tablespoon olive oil and remaining ¼ teaspoon salt. Position the chicken breasts on the pan so they are not overlapping and brush with about half of the barbecue sauce. Bake an additional 15 to 20 minutes, until an instant-read thermometer registers 165 degrees F. when inserted in the thickest part of a chicken breast.

Remove the pan from the oven and shred the chicken breasts using two forks. Toss the chicken with the remaining BBQ sauce. Divide between 4 bowls, along with the roasted sweet potatoes, broccoli, and onions, and serve immediately.

Per Serving: Calories 447 | **Fat** 13g | **Carb** 53g | **Fiber** 8g | **Sugar** 25g | **Protein** 34g

EGG ROLLS IN A BOWL

Prep time: 15 minutes | Cook time: 20 minutes | Total time: 35 minutes | Serves: 4

---

2 tablespoons sesame oil

2 tablespoons olive oil

1 tablespoon rice wine vinegar

1 tablespoon lower-sodium soy sauce

1 pound ground chicken

½ teaspoon ground black pepper

6 cups coleslaw mix

8 green onions, chopped

In a large skillet over low heat, whisk together the sesame oil, olive oil, rice wine vinegar, and soy sauce.

Add ground chicken. Break apart and cook ground chicken in sauce until cooked through, about 12 minutes. Add pepper and stir to combine.

Stir in coleslaw mix and cook just until cabbage and carrots start to become tender, about 3 minutes. If you cook it too long, the vegetables will turn mushy. Garnish with chopped green onions and serve.

Per Serving: Calories 239 | **Fat** 23g | **Carb** 4g | **Fiber** 3g | **Sugar** 14g | **Protein** 36.5g

WHITE BEAN CHICKEN CHILI

Prep time: 5 minutes | Cook time: 15 minutes | Total time: 20 minutes | Serves: 4

2 cups lower-sodium chicken broth

2 cups cooked, shredded chicken

2 (15-ounce) cans great northern beans, drained and rinsed

2 cups mild salsa verde

2 teaspoons ground cumin

1 avocado, diced

2 tablespoons freshly chopped cilantro

In a large stock pot set over medium-high heat, combine chicken broth, cooked chicken, beans, salsa verde, and cumin. Bring mix to a boil, reduce heat to low, and simmer 5 minutes to heat through.

Ladle chili into bowls and garnish each bowl with chopped avocado and cilantro.

Per Serving: Calories 238 | **Fat** 13g | **Carb** 16.5g | **Fiber** 7.5g | **Sugar** 0.5g | **Protein** 24.5g

MARINATED TURKEY BREAST

Prep time: 20 minutes (plus 4 hours marinating time) | Cook time: 30 minutes | Total time: 4 hours 50 minutes | Serves: 6

⅓ cup vegetable oil

⅓ cup soy sauce

2 tablespoons freshly squeezed lemon juice

2 tablespoons honey

1 teaspoon dried basil

2 cloves garlic, minced

½ teaspoon ground black pepper

1 (3-pound) boneless turkey breast half

In a large, resealable plastic bag, mix together vegetable oil, soy sauce, lemon juice, honey, basil, garlic, and black pepper. Add turkey breast to bag, seal bag, and let turkey marinate in refrigerator for at least 4 hours or overnight.

When ready to grill, heat grill to high and lightly oil it. Remove turkey breast from bag and discard marinade.

Place turkey breast on the grill. Close the lid, and grill turkey about 15 minutes on each side, until temperature registers 165 degrees F. on an instant-read thermometer inserted in the thickest part of the breast.

Per Serving: Calories 317 | Fat 6g | Carb 2g | Fiber 0g | Sugar 1g | Protein 60g

PROTEIN PENNE PASTA

Prep time: 10 minutes | Cook time: 20 minutes | Total time: 30 minutes | Serves: 5

8 ounces dry whole wheat penne pasta

1 pound ground turkey

2 cups sugar-free pasta sauce

½ cup 2% milkfat cottage cheese

½ cup plain nonfat Greek yogurt

1 teaspoon dried Italian seasoning

½ teaspoon garlic salt

4 tablespoons freshly shredded parmesan cheese

Cook pasta according to package directions. Drain and set aside until ready to serve.

Meanwhile, in a large skillet over medium heat, brown ground turkey until it is cooked through, about 12 minutes.

Stir in pasta sauce, cottage cheese, plain Greek yogurt, Italian seasoning, and garlic salt. Bring mixture to a simmer and cook until heated through, about 8 to 10 minutes.

Serve the sauce and meat mixture over penne pasta, and garnish with fresh shredded Parmesan cheese.

Per Serving: **Calories** 409.5 | **Fat** 11.5g | **Carb** 46.5g | **Fiber** 4g | **Sugar** 9.5g | **Protein** 32g

GROUND TURKEY GYROS

Prep time: 1 hour | Cook time: 20 minutes | Total time: 1 hour 20 minutes | Serves: 6

1½ pounds lean ground turkey

½ small red onion, minced

Salt and pepper, to taste

2 teaspoons dried oregano

4 cloves garlic, minced

2 tablespoons tomato paste

4 tablespoons red wine vinegar

6 whole wheat pitas

Fresh Greek Relish

Tzatziki

Note: Prepare the Fresh Greek Relish and Tzatziki at least 1 hour ahead of time to allow the flavors to meld. If desired, prepare as many as 2 days ahead.

In a large skillet over medium-high heat, break apart and sauté ground turkey and onions until turkey is cooked through, about 10 minutes. Drain off excess grease and then season with salt and pepper to taste.

Reduce temperature to low. Add oregano, garlic, tomato paste, and red wine vinegar to skillet and stir until meat is coated with seasonings.

To serve, add meat, Relish, and Tzatziki to a pita and enjoy.

To cut back on carbs and calories, serve ground turkey and toppings over a bed of lettuce instead of on a pita.

Fresh Greek Relish

1 tablespoon olive oil

1 tablespoon red wine vinegar

2 Roma tomatoes, seeded and diced

1 English cucumber, seeded and diced

½ red onion, diced

Salt and pepper, to taste

In a medium bowl, gently mix olive oil, vinegar, tomatoes, cucumbers, and onions. Season with salt and pepper to taste. Cover tightly with plastic wrap and refrigerate at least 1 hour, or up to 2 days.

Per Serving: Calories 432 | **Fat** 14.5g | **Carb** 47g | **Fiber** 6.5g | **Sugar** 7.5g | **Protein** 32g

Tzatziki

1 cucumber, peeled and seeded

2 cups plain nonfat Greek yogurt, strained

2 cloves garlic, minced

1 teaspoon red wine vinegar

½ teaspoon lemon juice

¼ teaspoon dried dill weed

Salt and pepper, to taste

Shred or grate cucumber into a small bowl. Blot cucumber shreds with a paper towel to soak up as much moisture as possible.

In a medium bowl, mix together shredded cucumbers, strained yogurt, garlic, vinegar, and lemon juice. Add dill and salt and pepper to taste. Cover tightly with plastic wrap and refrigerate at least 1 hour, or up to 2 days.

ITALIAN TURKEY SAUSAGE AND MINESTRONE SOUP

Prep time: 15 minutes | Cook time: 30 minutes | Total time: 45 minutes | Serves: 6

---

1 pound ground Italian turkey sausage

4 cups lower-sodium beef broth

2 cups water

2 (8-ounce) cans tomato sauce

1 (14.5-ounce) can petite diced tomatoes

1 (15.5-ounce) can red kidney beans, drained and rinsed

1½ cups diced celery

1½ cups diced carrots

1 teaspoon onion powder

1 teaspoon garlic salt

3 tablespoons Italian seasoning

10 ounces whole wheat shell pasta

½ cup shredded Parmesan cheese

In a large skillet over medium heat, break apart and brown sausage until fully cooked, about 12 minutes. Drain off excess grease.

In a large stock pot, combine beef broth, water, tomato sauce, diced tomatoes, kidney beans, celery, carrots, onion salt, garlic salt, and Italian seasoning. Bring to a simmer over medium heat and maintain the simmer until veggies become tender, about 20 minutes.

In a separate pot, cook pasta according to package directions. When noodles are done, add to soup and stir in cooked sausage. Cook several minutes to help flavors meld.

Served topped with shredded Parmesan cheese.

Per Serving: **Calories** 370 | **Fat** 10.5g | **Carb** 43.5g | **Fiber** 6.5g | **Sugar** 9g | **Protein** 24g

GARLIC STEAK KABOBS

Prep time: 10 minutes | Marinating time: 1 hour to overnight | Cook time: 10 minutes | Total time: 1 hour 20 minutes or longer | Yields: 8 kabobs

---

2 (3-ounce) chuck steaks, cut into 1-inch chunks

2 tablespoons olive oil

1 tablespoon crushed garlic

½ teaspoon ground black pepper

¼ cup Worcestershire sauce

16 large cremini mushrooms

1 green bell pepper, cut into large chunks

1 medium red onion, cut into chunks

In a large, resealable plastic bag, combine steak pieces, olive oil, crushed garlic, pepper, and Worcestershire sauce. Seal and toss bag to coat steak pieces. Refrigerate at least 1 hour or overnight.

When ready to prepare kabobs, soak 8 wooden skewers in water for at least 20 minutes to prevent them from burning on the grill. Preheat grill to medium-high.

Thread meat and vegetables onto skewers and grill 5 to 7 minutes. Rotate kabobs and grill an additional 2 to 3 minutes or until meat is cooked to your liking.

Per Serving (2 kabobs): **Calories** 226 | **Fat** 13g | **Carb** 11g | **Fiber** 2g | **Sugar** 7.2g | **Protein** 16.8g

FAJITA STEAK KABOBS

Prep time: 20 minutes | Cook time: 10 minutes | Total time: 30 minutes | Yields: 16 kabobs

2 pounds sirloin steak, cubed

2 tablespoons olive oil

1 tablespoon chili powder

2 teaspoons ground cumin

1 teaspoon salt

½ teaspoon ground black pepper

½ teaspoon paprika

¼ teaspoon garlic powder

¼ teaspoon onion powder

1 red bell pepper, cut into chunks

1 green bell pepper, cut into chunks

1 yellow bell pepper, cut into chunks

1 onion, cut into chunks

1 recipe Avocado Sour Cream

If using wooden skewers, soak 16 skewers in water 20 minutes before threading kabobs. This will prevent the wood from burning. Preheat grill to high.

Place steak cubes in a medium mixing bowl and toss with olive oil to coat; set aside.

In a small bowl, combine chili powder, cumin, salt, pepper, paprika, garlic powder, and onion powder. Sprinkle seasoning on top of steak and toss to coat; set aside.

Thread steak, peppers, and onions onto skewers, alternating between meat and vegetables. Grill 5 to 7 minutes. Rotate kabobs and grill an additional 2 to 3 minutes or until meat is cooked to your liking.

Serve with Avocado Sour Cream, for dipping.

Avocado Sour Cream

2 avocados, halved and pitted

1 cup sour cream

2 teaspoons minced garlic

2 tablespoons freshly squeezed lime juice

½ teaspoon salt

¼ teaspoon ground black pepper

In the jar of a blender, process avocado, sour cream, minced garlic, lime juice, salt, and pepper until smooth.

Per Serving (2 kabobs): **Calories** 434 | **Fat** 26.8g | **Carb** 12.4g | **Fiber** 4.8g | **Sugar** 3.4g | **Protein** 37.2g

SALISBURY STEAK MEATBALLS

Prep time: 25 minutes | Cook time: 6 hours | Total time: 6 hours 25 minutes | Serves: 6

---

1 (8-ounce) package fresh sliced mushrooms, divided

½ pound 93% lean ground beef

½ pound 93% lean ground turkey

1 onion, chopped and divided

3 tablespoons tomato paste, divided

1 large egg

½ cup old-fashioned rolled oats

Salt and pepper, to taste

1 (14-ounce) can lower-sodium beef broth, divided

2 tablespoons all-purpose flour

2 teaspoons Worcestershire sauce

3 tablespoons olive oil

2 tablespoons freshly chopped parsley (optional)

1 (20-ounce) package frozen mashed cauliflower, prepared according to package directions

Chop ½ cup of the sliced mushrooms. In a large mixing bowl, combine the ½ cup chopped sliced mushrooms, the ground beef, ground turkey, half of the chopped onions, 2 tablespoons of the tomato paste, egg, oatmeal, salt and pepper, and ¼ cup of the beef broth.

Thoroughly combine and form mixture into 1½-inch meatballs.

Heat oil in a large skillet over medium-high heat until oil ripples. Add meatballs, a few at a time, to the pan and cook a minute or 2, until first side is browned. Flip meatballs to brown the other side. Repeat until all meatballs are browned, but not cooked through.

Transfer browned meatballs to slow cooker.

In a small bowl, whisk together flour, remaining beef broth, remaining onions, remaining tomato paste, and Worcestershire sauce.

Top meatballs with remaining sliced mushrooms and pour sauce over the top.

Cover and cook on low for 6 hours.

Serve over cooked mashed cauliflower and, if desired, sprinkle with fresh parsley.

Per Serving: Calories 304 | **Fat** 17g | **Carb** 16.5g | **Fiber** 3.5g | **Sugar** 5.2g | **Protein** 21g

EASY MARINATED PORK CHOPS

Prep time: 5 minutes | Marinating time: 6 hours | Cook time: 10 minutes | Total time: 6 hours 15 minutes | Serves: 6

¾ cup vegetable oil

⅓ cup reduced-sodium soy sauce

¼ cup apple cider vinegar

2 tablespoons Worcestershire sauce

1 tablespoon freshly squeezed lemon juice

1 tablespoon Dijon mustard

Salt and pepper, to taste

1 teaspoon dried parsley

1 clove garlic, minced

6 (3-ounce) pork chops, cut about ¾-inch thick

In a large, resealable plastic bag, mix together oil, soy sauce, vinegar, Worcestershire sauce, lemon juice, Dijon mustard, salt and pepper to taste, parsley, and garlic. Add pork chops to bag, seal bag, and let chops marinate for at least 6 hours. The longer the chops marinate, the more tender and flavorful they will be.

When ready to grill, preheat grill to medium. Remove chops from bag and discard marinade.

Grill pork chops 4 to 5 minutes on each side, until temperature registers 145 degrees F. on an instant-read thermometer inserted in the thickest part of the chops.

Per Serving: Calories 256 | **Fat** 15g | **Carb** 2.5g | **Fiber** 0g | **Sugar** 1.5g | **Protein** 27.5g

TERIYAKI PORK STIR FRY

Prep time: 15 minutes | Cook time: 15 minutes | Total time: 30 minutes | Serves: 8

2 tablespoons olive oil, divided

2 cups broccoli florets

2 cups chopped fresh pineapple

1 red bell pepper, seeded and diced

1 green bell pepper, seeded and diced

1 medium onion, chopped

Salt and pepper, to taste

1 (1-pound) pork tenderloin, cubed

1 cup jarred teriyaki sauce, such as Kikkoman Teriyaki Marinade and Sauce

6 cups hot, cooked rice

Sesame seeds, for garnishing (optional)

Heat 1 tablespoon of the oil in a large skillet over medium-high heat until oil ripples. Add broccoli florets, pineapple, peppers, and onions and cook until vegetables are crisp-tender, about 6 minutes.

Season with salt and pepper to taste.

Remove vegetables and pineapple from the pan, place on a plate, and set aside.

Heat remaining tablespoon oil over medium-high heat until oil ripples. Add cubed pork and brown until cooked through, about 6 to 8 minutes.

Return vegetables and pineapple to the pan and toss to combine.

Pour teriyaki sauce over top and cook until heated through, about 3 minutes.

Serve over hot, cooked rice and, if desired, garnish with sesame seeds.

Per Serving: Calories 367 | **Fat** 8.5g | **Carb** 47g | **Fiber** 2.5g | **Sugar** 9g | **Protein** 23g

HONEY DIJON SALMON

Prep time: 5 minutes | Cook time: 15 minutes | Total time: 20 minutes | Serves: 4

2 tablespoons honey

2 tablespoons Dijon mustard

2 tablespoons olive oil

1 tablespoon freshly squeezed lemon juice

1 tablespoon freshly chopped parsley

Salt and pepper, to taste

4 (4-ounce) salmon fillets

1 lemon, sliced (optional)

Preheat oven to 400 degrees F. Line a rimmed baking sheet with aluminum foil.

In a small bowl, mix together honey, Dijon mustard, olive oil, lemon juice, fresh parsley, and salt and pepper to taste.

Place salmon fillets, skin side down, on prepared baking sheet. Brush the tops of the fillets with the honey mustard mixture.

Bake 12 to 15 minutes, until salmon is opaque and flakes easily with a fork. Garnish with a slice of lemon, if desired.

Per Serving: Calories 249 | **Fat** 14.5g | **Carb** 9.5g | **Fiber** 0.5g | **Sugar** 9g | **Protein** 22.5g

LEMON-GARLIC SALMON

Prep time: 10 minutes | Cook time: 12 minutes | Total time: 22 minutes | Serves: 4

4 (6-ounce) salmon fillets

Salt and pepper, to taste

1 tablespoon olive oil

2 tablespoons butter

4 cloves garlic, minced

¼ cup lower-sodium chicken broth

¼ cup freshly-squeezed lemon juice

2 tablespoons freshly chopped parsley

2 lemons, sliced thin

Pat fillets dry with paper towels and season both sides with salt and pepper to taste.

Heat oil in a large nonstick pan over medium-high heat until oil begins to ripple but does not smoke. Place salmon fillets, skin side down, on hot pan and cook, without moving, 3 to 4 minutes, until fillets are crispy and golden. Carefully flip over fillets with a fish spatula or other thin spatula.

Cook 2 to 3 minutes on second side.

Push fillets to the edges of the pan. In the middle of the pan, melt butter until foamy. Add garlic and sauté 30 seconds, until fragrant. Stir in chicken broth, lemon juice, and a pinch of salt. Move fillets back to the center of the pan so they are cooking in the sauce.

Reduce heat to low and let sauce simmer about 3 minutes. To serve, plate salmon, top each fillet with 1 or 2 lemon slices, sprinkle with parsley, and spoon some of the sauce from the pan over the top.

Per Serving: Calories 332.5 | **Fat** 20g | **Carb** 2.5g | **Fiber** 0g | **Sugar** 0.5g | **Protein** 34.5g

SHRIMP PROTEIN BOWLS WITH MANGO SALSA

Prep time: 15 minutes | Cook time: 10 minutes | Total time: 25 minutes | Serves: 4

1 teaspoon garlic powder

1 teaspoon chili powder

1 tablespoon freshly squeezed lime juice

½ tablespoon olive oil

12 ounces shrimp, peeled and deveined

1 recipe Mango Salsa

1 avocado, sliced

4 cups spinach

1 cup shredded carrots

1 cup shredded red cabbage

2 cups cooked brown rice

In a large bowl, whisk together garlic powder, chili powder, lime juice, and olive oil. Add shrimp and toss gently until all the shrimp have been coated. Transfer shrimp to a large skillet over medium heat and cook, stirring occasionally until slightly pink and opaque, about 3 to 4 minutes. Remove from heat and set aside.

To assemble shrimp bowls, place equal amounts of the mango salsa, shrimp, avocado, spinach, carrots, cabbage, and rice in each bowl. Serve immediately.

Mango Salsa

1 large ripe mango, diced

¼ small red onion, diced

½ red bell pepper, diced

1 finely diced tablespoon jalapeno pepper

1 tablespoon freshly chopped cilantro

1 tablespoon freshly squeezed lime juice

Pinch salt

In a medium bowl, mix together mangoes, onions, peppers, and cilantro. Toss with lime juice and then season with a pinch of salt to taste. Use immediately in Shrimp Protein Bowls or store refrigerated in an airtight container for 2 to 3 days.

Per Serving: Calories 356 | **Fat** 14g | **Carb** 36.5g | **Fiber** 7g | **Sugar** 9.5g | **Protein** 24g

CAULIFLOWER CRUST PIZZA

Prep time: 20 minutes | Cook time: 18 minutes | Total time: 38 minutes | Serves: 4

2 (10-ounce) bags frozen riced cauliflower

½ teaspoon salt

2 teaspoons Italian seasoning

1 teaspoon garlic powder

1 cup shredded Parmesan cheese

2½ cups shredded 2% milk mozzarella cheese

2 large eggs

¾ cup pizza sauce

Pepperoni slices (optional)

1 green bell pepper, sliced (optional)

Sliced mushrooms (optional)

Sliced olives (optional)

Note: Optional toppings are not included in the nutrition information.

Preheat oven to 425 degrees F. Line 2 baking sheets with parchment paper.

Steam cauliflower according to package directions. Cool slightly. Lay out a cheesecloth or tea towel on the counter and transfer cauliflower to towel. Wrap up cauliflower and wring out as much moisture as possible. Don't worry about mashing the cauliflower; it will be mashed when mixed together to form a crust.

In a large bowl, combine cauliflower, salt, Italian seasoning, garlic powder, Parmesan cheese, 1 cup of the mozzarella cheese, and eggs. Mix until well combined.

Separate dough into 2 halves. Flatten each half into an 8-inch circle on one of the prepared pans. Bake 10 minutes, until the top of the crust begins to turn golden brown.

Remove from oven and top each crust with pizza sauce and remaining mozzarella cheese. Finish off with your favorite pizza toppings, if desired.

Return to the oven and bake 6 to 8 minutes, until cheese has melted and begins to bubble. Slice each pizza into fourths and serve.

Per Serving (2 slices): **Calories** 177 | **Fat** 9.5g | **Carb** 10g | **Fiber** 2g | **Sugar** 26.5g | **Protein** 14g

PIZZA-STUFFED ZUCCHINI BOATS

Prep time: 10 minutes | Cook time: 18 minutes | Total time: 28 minutes | Yields: 8 Zucchini Boats

4 medium zucchini

½ cup marinara sauce

1 cup shredded 2% milk mozzarella cheese

¼ cup sliced mushrooms

¼ cup mini pepperonis

¼ cup diced green bell pepper

¼ cup diced onion

¼ cup sliced olives

Preheat oven to 400 degrees F.

Wash zucchini and cut in half lengthwise. Use a spoon to scrape out the seeds and pulp in the center of each zucchini half and pat dry with a paper towel.

Lay zucchini, cut side up, on a large, rimmed baking sheet.

Spread marinara sauce evenly between zucchini.

Top with equal portions shredded mozzarella, mushrooms, pepperonis, green pepper, onions, and olives.

Bake 12 to 18 minutes, until cheese is melted and zucchini is tender.

Per Serving (1 Zucchini Boat): **Calories** 107.5 | **Fat** 7g | **Carb** 5.5g | **Fiber** 1.5g | **Sugar** 3.5g | **Protein** 6g

side dishes

PARMESAN CRUSTED ASPARAGUS

Prep time: 10 minutes | Cook time: 20 minutes | Total time: 30 minutes | Serves: 6

1 pound asparagus, ends trimmed

Nonstick cooking spray

¼ cup shredded Parmesan cheese

Salt and pepper, to taste

1 cup garlic croutons

Preheat oven to 400 degrees F. Coat a 9x13-inch baking pan with nonstick cooking spray.

Place asparagus in prepared pan. Generously spray nonstick cooking spray on top of asparagus.

Sprinkle Parmesan cheese in an even layer on top of asparagus.

Season with salt and pepper to taste.

Place croutons in a resealable plastic bag, seal, and crush with a rolling pin until fine crumbs form.

Sprinkle crouton crumbs on top of asparagus and spray again with nonstick cooking spray.

Bake 15 to 20 minutes, or until crumb topping is golden brown and asparagus can be easily pierced with a fork.

Per Serving: Calories 124 | **Fat** 6g | **Carb** 10g | **Fiber** 1.5g | **Sugar** 1.5g | **Protein** 9.5g

HONEY-DIJON BRUSSELS SPROUTS

Prep time: 10 minutes | Cook time: 20 minutes | Total time: 30 minutes | Serves: 6

1½ pounds Brussels sprouts, halved

1 tablespoon olive oil

Salt and pepper, to taste

1½ tablespoons Dijon mustard

1½ tablespoons honey

Onion powder, to taste

Preheat oven to 425 degrees F. Line a rimmed baking sheet with aluminum foil.

Place sprouts on prepared baking sheet. Drizzle with olive oil and season with salt and pepper. Bake 20 to 25 minutes, until browned and tender, flipping halfway through the cooking time.

In a medium bowl, stir together mustard, honey, and onion powder.

Remove sprouts from baking sheet and toss with mustard mixture. Serve warm.

Per Serving: Calories 88 | **Fat** 3g | **Carb** 15g | **Fiber** 4.5g | **Sugar** 7g | **Protein** 4g

HONEY ROASTED CARROTS

Prep time: 5 minutes | Cook time: 30 minutes | Total time: 35 minutes | Serves: 6

1 pound baby carrots

3 tablespoons olive oil

3 tablespoons honey

Salt and pepper, to taste

Preheat oven to 400 degrees F. Line a baking sheet with foil and spray lightly with nonstick cooking spray.

Place carrots in a large, resealable plastic bag.

Pour olive oil over carrots, seal bag, and shake until carrots are evenly coated in oil.

Spread the carrots in a single layer on baking sheet.

Drizzle the honey over the carrots and season with salt and pepper, as desired.

Bake for 25 to 30 minutes, or until carrots are tender.

Per Serving: Calories 118 | **Fat** 7g | **Carb** 15g | **Fiber** 2g | **Sugar** 12.5g | **Protein** 0.5g

OVEN-ROASTED GREEN BEANS

Prep time: 5 minutes | Cook time: 25 minutes | Total time: 30 minutes | Serves: 6

2 pounds fresh green beans, trimmed

2 tablespoons olive oil

1 teaspoon salt

½ teaspoon ground black pepper

Preheat oven to 400 degrees F. Line large baking sheet with aluminum foil and spray lightly with nonstick cooking spray.

Spread beans in a single layer on a large baking sheet and drizzle with olive oil.

Sprinkle with salt and pepper. Using your hands (or a large spatula), lightly toss beans until they are coated with oil and seasonings. Spread beans back out in a single layer.

Cook 20 to 25 minutes, or until beans are tender and start getting brown spots on the outside.

Per Serving: Calories 87 | **Fat** 5g | **Carb** 11g | **Fiber** 5g | **Sugar** 2g | **Protein** 3g

ITALIAN PEAS

Prep time: 5 minutes | Cook time: 11 minutes | Total time: 16 minutes | Serves: 6

2 tablespoons olive oil

1 onion, minced

2 teaspoons minced garlic

1 (12-ounce) bag frozen peas

2 tablespoons lower-sodium chicken broth

Salt and pepper, to taste

Heat olive oil in a large skillet over medium heat until oil begins to ripple. Add onions and garlic and sauté until onions are soft and clear, about 7 minutes.

Stir in peas and chicken broth. Reduce temperature, cover, and simmer 4 to 5 minutes, until peas are soft and heated through.

Season with salt and pepper to taste. Serve immediately.

Per Serving: Calories 93 | **Fat** 5g | **Carb** 10g | **Fiber** 3.5g | **Sugar** 3.5g | **Protein** 3g

MAPLE-PECAN ROASTED ACORN SQUASH

Prep time: 10 minutes | Cook time: 1 hour 10 minutes | Total time: 1 hour 20 minutes | Serves: 4

2 acorn squash

3 tablespoons butter, softened

½ cup brown sugar

½ cup pure maple syrup

¼ cup chopped pecans

Preheat oven to 400 degrees F. Line a baking sheet with aluminum foil and spray with nonstick cooking spray.

Prep the squash by cutting it in half, scooping out the seeds, and scoring the middles with a paring knife.

Spread butter over squash, sprinkle with brown sugar, and drizzle with maple syrup.

Bake 1 hour, and then remove from oven and spoon juices that have fallen into the middle of the squash over outside of squash. Top with chopped pecans.

Return to oven and bake 10 more minutes.

Per Serving: Calories 281 | **Fat** 11.5g | **Carb** 46g | **Fiber** 4g | **Sugar** 22.5g | **Protein** 2.5g

ROASTED HONEY-CINNAMON BUTTERNUT SQUASH

Prep time: 10 minutes | Cook time: 40 minutes | Total time: 50 minutes | Serves: 6

1 (3-pound) butternut squash, peeled, seeded, and cubed (about 7 cups)

2 tablespoons olive oil

3 tablespoons honey

1 teaspoon ground cinnamon

Salt and pepper, to taste

Preheat oven to 425 degrees F. Line a rimmed baking sheet with aluminum foil and coat with non-stick cooking spray.

In a large bowl, toss squash with olive oil, honey, and cinnamon until squash is lightly coated.

Spread squash in a single layer on prepared baking sheet.

Roast 40 minutes or until squash reaches desired tenderness.

Top with salt and pepper and serve.

Per Serving: Calories 168 | **Fat** 5g | **Carb** 34g | **Fiber** 7g | **Sugar** 13.5g | **Protein** 2g

BAKED PARMESAN SPAGHETTI SQUASH

Prep time: 10 minutes | Cook time: 1 hour 20 minutes | Total time: 1 hour 30 minutes | Serves: 4

1 (3-pound) spaghetti squash

⅔ cup butter, melted

1 teaspoon garlic salt

½ teaspoon ground black pepper

½ teaspoon Italian seasoning

¼ teaspoon salt

½ cup grated Parmesan cheese

2 sprigs parsley (optional)

Preheat oven to 350 degrees F. Pour 2 cups water in a 9x13-inch baking dish.

Place uncut spaghetti squash in water and cover dish tightly with aluminum foil.

Bake 1 hour.

Remove from oven, drain water out of pan, and transfer squash to a cutting board to cool. Let squash cool about 20 minutes, until it's easier to handle.

Slice squash into 4 pieces and scoop out the seeds. Return cut slices to baking dish.

In a small bowl, stir together melted butter, garlic salt, pepper, Italian seasoning, and salt.

Brush the butter mixture onto each slice. Sprinkle each slice with 2 tablespoons shredded Parmesan cheese.

Return squash to oven and bake about 20 minutes, until cheese has melted into the spaghetti squash. Garnish with parsley if desired.

Per Serving: Calories 330 | **Fat** 34.4g | **Carb** 2.8g | **Fiber** 0g | **Sugar** 0.5g | **Protein** 4g

CHEESY ZUCCHINI STICKS

Prep time: 10 minutes | Cook time: 13 minutes | Total time: 23 minutes | Serves: 6

5 medium zucchini

4 tablespoons butter, melted

2 teaspoons minced garlic

Garlic salt, to taste

¾ cup shredded 2% milk Mozzarella cheese

Preheat oven to 350 degrees F. Line a rimmed baking sheet with aluminum foil.

Cut zucchini into long, thick wedges and line up on prepared baking sheet.

In a small bowl, stir together melted butter and garlic. Brush the garlic-butter mixture onto zucchini.

Sprinkle with garlic salt to taste and shredded Mozzarella cheese.

Bake 11 to 13 minutes, until the cheese starts to brown and zucchini are fork tender. Serve warm.

Per Serving: **Calories** 110 | **Fat** 8.5g | **Carb** 7g | **Fiber** 2g | **Sugar** 3g | **Protein** 3.5g

GARLIC-LIME SWEET POTATO FRIES

Prep time: 10 minutes | Cook time: 25 minutes | Total time: 35 minutes | Serves: 4

3 yellow sweet potatoes

1½ tablespoons olive oil

Juice of 1 lime

1 tablespoon minced garlic

2 tablespoons finely chopped cilantro

½ teaspoon salt

½ teaspoon ground black pepper

Preheat oven to 425 degrees F.

Cut sweet potatoes in half lengthwise, and then slice each half into several wedges. Line wedges on a large, rimmed baking sheet. Drizzle olive oil and lime juice over potatoes and then sprinkle with garlic, cilantro, salt, and pepper. Use your hands to toss the potatoes until evenly coated in oil and seasonings.

Bake 20 to 25 minutes, or until fries begin to turn crisp and golden brown.

Per Serving: Calories 187 | **Fat** 5.5g | **Carb** 34g | **Fiber** 5g | **Sugar** 0.5g | **Protein** 2g

EASY BAKED TACO FRIES

Prep time: 15 minutes | Cook time: 30 minutes | Total time: 45 minutes | Serves: 6

6 russet potatoes

2 tablespoons olive oil

1 tablespoon chili powder

¼ teaspoon garlic powder

¼ teaspoon onion powder

¼ teaspoon dried oregano

½ teaspoon paprika

1½ teaspoons ground cumin

1 teaspoon salt

1 teaspoon ground black pepper

Preheat oven to 450 degrees F. Spray a rimmed baking sheet with nonstick cooking spray.

Scrub potatoes and dry with paper towels. Cut each potato in half lengthwise, then cut each half into 4 to 6 wedges.

Place cut potatoes in a large, resealable plastic bag and pour olive oil on top.

Seal bag and shake until potatoes are coated in olive oil.

In a small bowl, combine chili powder, garlic powder, onion powder, dried oregano, paprika, cumin, salt, and pepper.

Pour spice mixture into bag, seal, and shake to coat again. Spread potatoes out in an even layer on the prepared pan.

Bake 25 to 30 minutes, turning halfway through, until wedges are golden brown and crisp on the outside.

Per Serving: **Calories** 337 | **Fat** 5g | **Carb** 65.5g | **Fiber** 7.5g | **Sugar** 4.5g | **Protein** 8g

3-INGREDIENT AVOCADO SALAD

Prep time: 10 minutes | Total time: 10 minutes | Serves: 4

---

1 cup halved cherry tomatoes

2 avocados, diced

1 (6.5-ounce) jar chopped marinated artichoke hearts

Gently fold halved tomatoes and diced avocado together in a small mixing bowl.

Drain marinated artichoke hearts, reserving some of the marinade.

Fold chopped artichoke hearts into tomatoes and diced avocado. Drizzle with some of the reserved marinade as desired.

Per Serving: Calories 195 | **Fat** 16.5 | **Carb** 14g | **Fiber** 6.5g | **Sugar** 1.5g | **Protein** 2g

HEALTHY BROCCOLI SALAD

Prep time: 10 minutes | Chilling time: 2 hours | Total time: 2 hours 10 minutes | Serves: 6

8 cups broccoli florets

2 apples, unpeeled and diced

¼ cup diced sweet onion

½ cup Craisins

2 tablespoons honey

6 tablespoons apple cider vinegar

2 tablespoons Dijon mustard

1 tablespoon canola oil

½ teaspoon fresh ground black pepper

Salt, to taste

In a large bowl, mix together broccoli florets, apples, onions, and Craisins.

In a medium bowl, whisk together honey, vinegar, mustard, canola oil, pepper, and salt to taste.

Pour dressing over broccoli mixture and toss well. Cover bowl and chill in refrigerator at least 2 hours before serving to let the flavors meld together.

Per Serving: Calories 143 | **Fat** 3g | **Carb** 26.5g | **Fiber** 5g | **Sugar** 18.5g | **Protein** 4g

PEAR AND BLUE CHEESE SALAD

Prep time: 10 minutes | Total time: 10 minutes | Serves: 8

1 (10-ounce) package spring salad mix

1 red onion, thinly sliced

1 Bartlett pear, diced

½ cup candied pecans, such as Emerald Glazed Pecans

½ cup reduced-fat blue cheese crumbles

¼ cup pure maple syrup

⅓ cup apple cider vinegar

½ cup light mayonnaise

2 tablespoons brown sugar

1 teaspoon salt

¼ teaspoon ground black pepper

¼ cup olive oil

Place salad in a large bowl and toss with onion, pears, pecans, and blue cheese crumbles.

In the jar of a blender, add maple syrup, vinegar, mayonnaise, brown sugar, salt, pepper, and olive oil. Process until smooth.

Pour dressing over salad and toss to coat.

Per Serving: Calories 209 | **Fat** 14.5g | **Carb** 20g | **Fiber** 1.5g | **Sugar** 14g | **Protein** 3g

SPINACH, CUCUMBER, AND STRAWBERRY SALAD

Prep time: 15 minutes | Total time: 15 minutes | Serves: 6

10 packed cups baby spinach

1½ cups chopped strawberries

3 small cucumbers, sliced

⅓ cup chopped pecans

¼ cup feta cheese crumbles

1 recipe Balsamic Vinaigrette

In a large bowl, toss together spinach, strawberries, cucumbers, pecans, and feta cheese. Toss with Balsamic Vinaigrette, or serve the vinaigrette on the side, and enjoy!

Balsamic Vinaigrette

⅓ cup extra virgin olive oil

⅓ cup balsamic vinegar

½ teaspoon crushed garlic

1 teaspoon ground mustard

¼ teaspoon salt

⅛ teaspoon ground black pepper

Process all ingredients in a blender until smooth. Store in the refrigerator in an airtight container until ready to use. Keeps up to 1 week; just shake well before using.

Per Serving: Calories 163 | **Fat** 13.5g | **Carb** 10g | **Fiber** 2g | **Sugar** 5g | **Protein** 3g

CREAMY YOGURT AND FRESH FRUIT SALAD

Prep time: 15 minutes | Total time: 15 minutes | Serves: 6

2 cups sliced strawberries

2 fresh peaches, peeled and diced

2 medium bananas, sliced

2 cups red seedless grapes

2 tablespoons freshly squeezed lime juice

1 (8-ounce) container nonfat vanilla yogurt

2 teaspoons freshly squeezed lemon juice

½ teaspoon vanilla extract

In a large bowl toss strawberries, peaches, bananas, and grapes with lime juice. This will keep the fruit from browning.

In a separate small bowl, mix together yogurt, lemon juice, and vanilla. Pour yogurt mixture over fruit and fold gently until combined.

Per Serving: Calories 137 | **Fat** 1g | **Carb** 30g | **Fiber** 3g | **Sugar** 23g | **Protein** 3.5g

BLACK BEAN AND CORN SALSA

Prep time: 10 minutes | Total time: 10 minutes | Serves: 6

---

1 (15-ounce) can corn, drained

1 (15-ounce) can black beans, drained and rinsed

1 (10-ounce) can RoTel Diced Tomatoes and Green Chilies

1 bunch cilantro, minced

1 red onion, minced

3 green onions, diced

1 red bell pepper, diced

2 tablespoons freshly squeezed lime juice

½ teaspoon minced garlic

1 jalapeño, seeded and minced

Ground cumin, to taste

In a large mixing bowl, combine all ingredients until fully incorporated. Store, covered, in the refrigerator until ready to serve.

Per Serving: Calories 125.5 | **Fat** 1g | **Carb** 27g | **Fiber** 6.5g | **Sugar** 4g | **Protein** 6.5g

CAPRESE SALSA

Prep time: 10 minutes | Total time: 10 minutes | Serves: 4

---

2 cups chopped cherry tomatoes

4 ounces part-skim mozzarella pearls

1 tablespoon fresh chopped basil

½ red onion, diced

½ teaspoon salt

½ teaspoon ground black pepper

2 tablespoons olive oil

1½ tablespoons balsamic vinegar

In a large bowl, toss together chopped cherry tomatoes, mozzarella pearls, basil, red onions, salt, and pepper.

Drizzle with olive oil and balsamic vinegar and toss until coated.

Serve with your favorite pita chips or tortilla chips.

Per Serving: Calories 126 | **Fat** 8g | **Carb** 6g | **Fiber** 1.5g | **Sugar** 3.5g | **Protein** 8g

SPANISH CAULIFLOWER RICE

Prep time: 5 minutes | Cook time: 15 minutes | Total time: 20 minutes | Serves: 6

1 tablespoon olive oil

½ cup diced onion

1 (12-ounce) bag frozen riced cauliflower

2 tablespoons tomato paste

1 (10-ounce) can RoTel Diced Tomatoes and Green Chilies, drained

1 teaspoon ground cumin

½ teaspoon chili powder

1 teaspoon minced garlic

Salt and pepper, to taste

Heat oil in a large skillet over medium heat until oil ripples. Add diced onions and sauté until tender, about 5 minutes.

Increase heat to medium-high. Add frozen riced cauliflower, tomato paste, tomatoes, cumin, chili powder, garlic, and salt and pepper to taste. Cook 6 to 8 minutes, until the cauliflower is light and fluffy and the mixture is hot.

Serve warm.

Per Serving: Calories 56 | **Fat** 2.5g | **Carb** 7g | **Fiber** 2g | **Sugar** 3.5g | **Protein** 2g

JALAPEÑO-POPPER DEVILED EGGS

Prep time: 15 minutes | Total time: 15 minutes | Yields: 24 deviled eggs

12 hard-boiled eggs

2 tablespoons light mayonnaise

4 ounces light cream cheese, softened

2 tablespoons chopped jarred jalapeños

4 slices bacon, cooked crisp and crumbled

½ teaspoon onion powder

½ teaspoon garlic salt

2 fresh jalapeños, sliced thinly

Slice hard-boiled eggs lengthwise. Remove the yolk from each egg and transfer yolks to a medium bowl. Arrange whites on a serving platter and set aside.

Mash yolks lightly with a fork and then stir in mayonnaise, cream cheese, jarred jalapeños, bacon crumbles, onion powder, and garlic salt.

Spoon yolk mixture back into whites. Top each egg with a thin slice of fresh jalapeño.

Per Serving (1 deviled egg): **Calories** 70 | **Fat** 5.5g | **Carb** 1g | **Fiber** 0g | **Sugar** 0.5g | **Protein** 4.5g

3-INGREDIENT COTTAGE CHEESE RANCH DIP

Prep time: 5 minutes | Total time: 5 minutes | Serves: 15

2 cups 2% milkfat cottage cheese

1 cup nonfat plain Greek yogurt

1 (1-ounce) packet dry ranch dressing mix

Note: If you don't have a blender, you can mix all ingredients together in a bowl by hand. The dip won't be as creamy, and it will have a bumpy texture from the cottage cheese, but it will still be delicious!

In the jar of a blender, process cottage cheese and Greek yogurt until smooth.

Pour contents into a medium bowl and fold in dry ranch dressing packet. Mix until completely incorporated.

Serve with your favorite fresh vegetables.

Per Serving: Calories 45 | **Fat** 0.5g | **Carb** 2.5g | **Fiber** 0g | **Sugar** 1.5g | **Protein** 7g

snacks and desserts

HEALTHY PUMPKIN CHOCOLATE CHIP COOKIES

Prep time: 10 minutes | Cook time: 15 minutes | Total time: 25 minutes | Yields: 2 dozen cookies

1 (15-ounce) can pure pumpkin

½ cup unsweetened applesauce

½ cup granulated sugar

1 teaspoon vanilla extract

1 teaspoon baking soda

1 teaspoon baking powder

¼ teaspoon salt

2 teaspoons pumpkin pie spice

2 cups whole wheat flour

1 cup semisweet chocolate chips

Preheat oven to 350 degrees F. Line cookie sheets with parchment paper or spray with nonstick cooking spray.

In a large bowl, with an electric mixer, combine pumpkin, applesauce, sugar, and vanilla.

Add baking soda, baking powder, salt, pumpkin pie spice, and flour. Mix until well combined.

Fold in dark chocolate chips.

Drop by large, rounded tablespoons onto prepared baking sheets.

Bake 12 to 15 minutes or until cookies are just beginning to brown around the edges. Remove from oven and let the cookies cool on the baking sheet for two minutes before transferring to a wire rack to cool completely.

Per Serving (1 cookie): **Calories** 119 | **Fat** 4.3g | **Carb** 20.5g | **Fiber** 3.5g | **Sugar** 8.5g | **Protein** 2.5g

NO-BAKE CHOCOLATE PEANUT BUTTER COOKIES

Prep time: 5 minutes | Cook time: 10 minutes | Total time: 15 minutes | Serves: 14

¼ cup solid coconut oil

½ cup natural peanut butter, such as Smucker's Natural Creamy Peanut Butter

¼ cup honey

Dash salt

2 tablespoons unsweetened cocoa powder

1 teaspoon vanilla extract

1½ cups old-fashioned rolled oats

Line a rimmed baking sheet with waxed paper or parchment paper.

In a large saucepan over medium-low heat, combine coconut oil, peanut butter, honey, and salt. Stir slowly until ingredients are completely melted.

Stir in the cocoa powder and vanilla and mix until completely combined. Remove from heat and stir in the oats until all of the oats are coated in chocolate.

Drop 14 tablespoonfuls of the cookie mixture on the prepared pan.

Place cookie sheet in the fridge or freezer to allow cookies to set up completely. Transfer cookies to a resealable plastic bag and store in the refrigerator up to 1 week.

Per Serving (1 cookie): **Calories** 146 | **Fat** 9g | **Carb** 15g | **Fiber** 1.5g | **Sugar** 10.5g | **Protein** 3.5g

NO-BAKE PEANUT BUTTER CEREAL BARS

Prep time: 55 minutes | Total time: 55 minutes | Serves: 16

1¾ cups Rice Krispies Cereal

1½ cups old-fashioned rolled oats

¾ cup chopped peanuts or almonds

¾ cup natural peanut butter, such as
   Smucker's Natural Creamy Peanut Butter

½ cup honey

¼ cup coconut sugar

1 teaspoon vanilla extract

Line a 7x11-inch pan with aluminum foil, leaving several inches of foil hanging over the sides so that bars are easy to lift out.

In a large bowl combine cereal, oats, and chopped nuts.

In a medium, microwave-safe bowl, combine the peanut butter, honey, and coconut sugar. Stir until ingredients are thoroughly combined.

Place in microwave and heat 1 minute on high. Remove from microwave and stir until creamy and smooth. Return to the microwave and heat for another 30 seconds. Stir in vanilla.

Pour hot peanut butter mixture over the cereal mixture in the large bowl and stir well to coat cereal.

Place mixture into prepared pan and spread evenly over all. Press down well with the back of a wooden spoon.

Cool 30 to 45 minutes before cutting into bars.

Lift foil out of pan and slice into 16 bars.

Per Serving (1 bar): **Calories** 213.5 | **Fat** 10g | **Carb** 28.5g | **Fiber** 2.5g | **Sugar** 20g | **Protein** 6g

PEANUT BUTTER PROTEIN BARS

Prep time: 1 hour 10 minutes | Total time: 1 hour 10 minutes | Serves: 9

1½ cups quick cooking oats

½ cup shredded unsweetened coconut

½ cup natural peanut butter, such as
   Smucker's Natural Creamy Peanut Butter

¼ cup honey

¼ cup unsweetened applesauce

¼ cup chocolate protein powder

2 tablespoons chia seeds

1 teaspoon vanilla extract

½ cup mini semisweet chocolate chips

Lightly coat a 9x9-inch baking dish with non-stick cooking spray. In a large bowl, mix together oats, coconut, peanut butter, honey, applesauce, protein powder, chia seeds, and vanilla. Fold in chocolate chips.

Press mixture into prepared pan and refrigerate 1 to 2 hours, until firm.

Per Serving (1 bar): **Calories** 276 | **Fat** 13.5g | **Carb** 4.5g | **Fiber** 4g | **Sugar** 14.5g | **Protein** 10.5g

FUNFETTI PROTEIN BITES

Prep time: 15 minutes | Total time: 15 minutes | Serves: 6

2 tablespoons raw honey

4 tablespoons almond butter

1 teaspoon vanilla extract

⅓ cup vanilla protein powder

⅓ cup old-fashioned rolled oats

1 tablespoon rainbow sprinkles

In a small bowl, mix together honey, almond butter, and vanilla.

Fold in protein powder, oats, and sprinkles.

Add more oats or honey until mixture comes together easily. Shape into six balls. Place on a plate and freeze 1 hour.

Store, refrigerated, in airtight container up to 7 days.

Per Serving (1 Protein Bite): **Calories** 184 | **Fat** 8g | **Carb** 14.5g | **Fiber** 1.5g | **Sugar** 8.5g | **Protein** 13g

SKINNY FROZEN STRAWBERRY BITES

Prep time: 40 minutes | Total time: 40 minutes | Yields: 24 Strawberry Bites

1 cup pecan halves

⅓ cup unsweetened coconut flakes, plus more
  for garnishing

1 tablespoon honey

1 teaspoon olive oil

1 cup fresh strawberries

½ cup nonfat plain Greek yogurt

Coat a 24-cup mini muffin tin with nonstick cooking spray.

In the jar of a blender, combine the pecans, coconut, honey, and olive oil and process until fully combined.

Press the pecan mixture into each cup of the muffin tin to form miniature crusts.

Clean the blender jar and add strawberries. Process strawberries until pureed.

Pour the blended strawberries into a small bowl and fold in the Greek yogurt.

Spoon the strawberry mixture on top of the pecan crust, filling each cup just to the top.

Place the pan in the freezer 30 minutes to 1 hour. When ready to eat, use a knife to go around the edges of each bite and pop it out.

Serve immediately and enjoy.

Per Serving (1 Strawberry Bite): **Calories** 67 | **Fat** 6.5g | **Carb** 2g | **Fiber** 0.5g | **Sugar** 1.5g | **Protein** 0.5g

EASY BANANA COOKIES

Prep time: 10 minutes | Cook time: 12 minutes | Total time: 22 minutes | Yields: 12 cookies

---

2 medium ripe bananas, mashed

1 cup old-fashioned rolled oats

¼ cup mini dark chocolate chips

Preheat oven to 350 degrees F. Spray a cookie sheet with nonstick cooking spray.

In a medium bowl, stir together the mashed bananas and oats with a wooden spoon. Fold in chocolate chips.

Using a spoon or cookie scoop, scoop up the batter and place on the cookie sheet in 12 mounds. Bake 12 to 15 minutes, until tops are turning crisp and slightly brown.

Per Serving: Calories 63 | **Fat** 2g | **Carb** 12g | **Fiber** 2g | **Sugar** 4g | **Protein** 1g

FLOURLESS BANANA BREAD

Prep time: 5 minutes | Cook time: 30 minutes | Total time: 35 minutes | Serves: 10

3 medium ripe bananas, mashed

2 cups old-fashioned rolled oats

2 large eggs

¼ cup pure maple syrup

1 teaspoon baking soda

½ cup sugar-free chocolate chips

Preheat oven to 350 degrees F. Coat a 9x5-inch loaf pan with nonstick cooking spray.

In a large bowl, combine bananas, oats, eggs, syrup, and baking soda. Stir well.

Pour batter into prepared loaf pan.

Sprinkle sugar-free chocolate chips over the top.

Bake 30 to 35 minutes or until a toothpick inserted in the center comes out clean.

Let loaf cool completely in loaf pan then remove and store bread in an airtight container in the refrigerator.

Per Serving: **Calories** 158 | **Fat** 4g | **Carb** 28g | **Fiber** 3g | **Sugar** 11g | **Protein** 4g

BANANA SHEET CAKE

Prep time: 15 minutes | Cook time: 25 minutes | Total time: 40 minutes | Serves: 15

5 medium ripe bananas, mashed

¾ cup honey

½ cup unsweetened applesauce

2 large eggs

1 teaspoon vanilla extract

1½ teaspoons baking soda

½ teaspoon salt

½ teaspoon ground cinnamon

¼ teaspoon ground nutmeg

2 cups all-purpose flour

1 cup mini semisweet chocolate chips, divided

Preheat oven to 350 degrees F. Coat a 13x18-inch half sheet pan with nonstick cooking spray.

In a large bowl, stir together mashed bananas, honey, applesauce, eggs, and vanilla and mix until well combined.

Add baking soda, salt, cinnamon, nutmeg, and flour and stir until well combined.

Fold in ½ cup of the chocolate chips.

Spread batter evenly in prepared half sheet pan.

Sprinkle remaining ½ cup chocolate chips on top of cake and bake 20 to 25 minutes, or until the top is golden brown and the middle of the cake bounces back when touched lightly.

Per Serving: Calories 236 | **Fat** 6g | **Carb** 46g | **Fiber** 3g | **Sugar** 27.5g | **Protein** 3g

DARK-CHOCOLATE ZUCCHINI CAKE

Prep time: 10 minutes | Cook time: 35 minutes | Total time: 45 minutes | Serves: 9

1 cup natural peanut butter, such as Smucker's Natural Creamy Peanut Butter

⅓ cup honey

1 medium ripe banana, mashed

1 teaspoon vanilla extract

½ cup unsweetened cocoa powder

1 teaspoon baking soda

2 teaspoons ground cinnamon

¼ teaspoon salt

½ cup cacao nibs, such as Navitas Naturals Organic Cacao Nibs

2 cups shredded zucchini

Preheat oven to 350 degrees F. Spray a 9x9-inch baking dish with nonstick cooking spray.

In a large bowl, whisk together peanut butter, honey, banana, and vanilla. Stir in cocoa powder, baking soda, cinnamon, and salt until well combined. Fold in dark chocolate cocoa nibs and zucchini.

Transfer mixture to prepared pan and spread evenly.

Bake 35 to 40 minutes, until a toothpick inserted in the center of cake comes out almost clean.

Allow cake to completely cool before slicing and serving.

Per Serving: Calories 290 | **Fat** 20g | **Carb** 27.5g | **Fiber** 9.5g | **Sugar** 14g | **Protein** 10.5g

POWER-PACKED GRANOLA

Prep time: 10 minutes | Cook time: 30 minutes | Total time: 40 minutes | Yields: 13 half-cup servings

3 cups old-fashioned rolled oats

1 cup sliced almonds

1 cup chopped pecans

1 cup shredded unsweetened coconut

3 tablespoons chia seeds

2 tablespoons flax seeds

1 tablespoon ground cinnamon

½ teaspoon salt

¼ cup honey

3 tablespoons coconut oil, melted

½ teaspoon vanilla extract

Preheat oven to 300 degrees F. Line a large, rimmed baking sheet with parchment paper.

In a large bowl, mix together oats, almonds, pecans, coconut, chia seeds, flax seeds, cinnamon, and salt.

In a small bowl, whisk together honey, coconut oil, and vanilla, then pour over the oat mixture and stir until combined.

Spread granola evenly onto prepared baking sheet.

Bake 30 minutes, tossing mixture halfway through. Cool completely when done baking. Transfer to an airtight container and store at room temperature up to 2 weeks.

Per Serving (1/2 cup): **Calories** 283 | **Fat** 13.5g | **Carb** 35g | **Fiber** 7g | **Sugar** 7g | **Protein** 7.5g

STRAWBERRY-GRANOLA YOGURT BARK

Prep time: 1 hour 10 minutes | Total time: 1 hour 10 minutes | Serves: 12

1 (24-ounce) carton nonfat vanilla Greek yogurt

2 teaspoons honey

1 cup sliced strawberries

1 cup granola

Line a 9x13-inch baking dish with aluminum foil.

In a small bowl, mix together yogurt and honey. Spread mixture into the bottom of the prepared pan.

Distribute the strawberries and granola over the top of the yogurt, slightly pressing it into the yogurt with your hands.

Freeze 1 hour, or until completely frozen.

Remove from freezer and cut into 12 slices with a pizza cutter. Serve immediately, or store in freezer in a freezer-safe bag up to 30 days.

Per Serving: Calories 88 | **Fat** 6.5g | **Carb** 22g | **Fiber** 2.5g | **Sugar** 12g | **Protein** 8g

BAKED CINNAMON-APPLE CRISPS

Prep time: 10 minutes | Cook time: 1 hour 45 minutes | Total time: 1 hour 55 minutes | Serves: 4

---

3 Pink Lady or Gala apples

2 tablespoons ground cinnamon

Move oven rack to lowest position. Preheat oven to 225 degrees F. Line a large baking sheet with parchment paper.

Core apples and slice as thin as you can, about ⅛-inch thick.

Arrange the apple slices closely together on the parchment paper. Sprinkle evenly with cinnamon.

Place pan on the lowest oven rack and bake 50 minutes. Use a spatula to gently turn over the apple slices. Bake another 50 to 60 minutes. Keep an eye on the apples during the last 10 minutes of cooking to ensure they do not burn.

Cool completely. Apples will come out a bit soft but will crisp up as they cool.

Per Serving: Calories 68 | **Fat** 0g | **Carb** 19g | **Fiber** 5.5g | **Sugar** 12.5g | **Protein** 0g

RASPBERRY FROZEN YOGURT

Prep time: 15 minutes | Freezing time: 1 hour | Total time: 1 hour 15 minutes | Serves: 3

1½ cups fresh raspberries

1 (5.3-ounce) carton nonfat raspberry Greek yogurt

1 teaspoon honey

½ teaspoon lemon juice

Place raspberries, yogurt, honey, and lemon juice in the jar of a blender and process until smooth and well combined.

Transfer blended yogurt to an airtight container and freeze at least 1 hour.

Once frozen, spoon into bowls and serve.

Per Serving: Calories 83 | **Fat** 0.5g | **Carb** 16g | **Fiber** 4g | **Sugar** 4.5g | **Protein** 5g

STRAWBERRY DOLE WHIP

Prep time: 15 minutes | Freezing time: 2 hours | Total time: 2 hours 15 minutes | Serves: 4

3 cups frozen sliced strawberries

½ cup pineapple juice

½ cup unsweetened almond milk

1 tablespoon freshly squeezed lemon juice

In the jar of a blender, process strawberries, pineapple juice, almond milk, and lemon juice until smooth.

Transfer mixture to a large resealable plastic bag, seal, and place in the freezer for 2 hours.

Remove bag from freezer and snip off a bottom corner of the bag with a pair of sharp scissors. Squeeze the mixture into 4 clear glasses and serve immediately.

Per Serving: Calories 60 | **Fat** 0.5g | **Carb** 14g | **Fiber** 2.5g | **Sugar** 10g | **Protein** 0.5g

WATERMELON SORBET

Prep time: 15 minutes | Freezing time: 6 hours | Total time: 6 hours 15 minutes | Serves: 4

5 cups cubed watermelon

1 cup coconut milk

Juice of 1 lemon

1 teaspoon coconut extract

2 teaspoons freshly chopped mint

In the jar of a blender, process watermelon, coconut milk, lemon juice, and coconut extract until smooth.

Pour mixture into a 9x13-inch pan and place in the freezer until firm, about 4 hours.

Scoop frozen mixture from the pan and return to the blender.

Blend until smooth.

Return to the pan and freeze again, this time for about 2 hours.

Serve garnished with fresh mint and a splash of lemon juice.

Per Serving: Calories 251 | **Fat** 15g | **Carb** 31.1g | **Fiber** 3.g | **Sugar** 23.5g | **Protein** 3.5g

CHOCOLATE-COVERED STRAWBERRY PROTEIN SHAKE

Prep time: 3 minutes | Total time: 3 minutes | Yields: 2 (8-ounce) shakes

1 cup frozen or fresh strawberries, sliced

½ medium frozen banana

3 tablespoons chocolate protein powder

2 teaspoons honey

½ cup unsweetened almond milk

½ cup ice

In the jar of a blender, process strawberries, banana, protein powder, honey, and almond milk until well combined. Add ice and process again. Serve cold.

Per Serving (8-ounce smoothie): **Calories** 90 | **Fat** 2g | **Carb** 12.5g | **Fiber** 2g | **Sugar** 8.5g | **Protein** 5.5g

ABC CHOCOLATE PUDDING

Prep time: 10 minutes | Chilling time: 1 hour | Total time: 1 hour 10 minutes | Serves: 4

1 avocado

4 medium ripe bananas

5 tablespoons unsweetened cocoa powder

1 tablespoon honey

1 teaspoon vanilla extract

½ teaspoon salt

½ cup whipped cream (optional)

⅛ cup raspberries (optional)

Note: Optional toppings are not included in the nutrition information.

Slice avocado in half and remove the seed. Scoop avocado from the skin.

Place avocado, bananas, cocoa, honey, vanilla, and salt in the jar of a blender and process completely smooth, about 1 minute.

Pour pudding into 4 serving bowls. Cover each bowl with plastic wrap and chill in the refrigerator at least 1 hour.

If desired, served topped with whipped cream and raspberries.

Per Serving: Calories 287 | **Fat** 15.5g | **Carb** 40.5g | **Fiber** 8.5g | **Sugar** 19.5g | **Protein** 4g

CHOCOLATE-PEANUT BUTTER BANANA ICE CREAM

Prep time: 10 minutes | Freezing time: 2 hours to overnight | Total time: 2 hours 10 minutes | Serves: 4

6 medium ripe bananas

½ cup unsweetened almond milk

¼ cup powdered peanut butter, such as PB2 Powdered Peanut Butter

¼ cup unsweetened cocoa powder

2 teaspoons honey

Crushed peanuts (optional, for topping)

Natural peanut butter (optional, for topping)

Note: Optional toppings are not included in nutrition information.

Peel bananas and cut into ½-inch pieces. Place banana pieces on a baking sheet lined with waxed paper and freeze 2 hours.

Once bananas are frozen, transfer to the bowl of a food processor, add almond milk, and process until smooth.

Add peanut butter powder, cocoa powder, and honey and blend until just combined.

Enjoy immediately, topped with peanuts and a drizzle of melted peanut butter, if desired. To serve later, transfer to an airtight container and freeze up to 10 days. If frozen, the ice cream will look more like traditional hard ice cream.

Per Serving: Calories 230 | **Fat** 3g | **Carb** 51.5g | **Fiber** 8.5g | **Sugar** 25.5g | **Protein** 8g

SKINNY BANANA SPLIT

Prep time: 5 minutes | Total time: 5 minutes | Serves: 4

2 large bananas

2 cups nonfat vanilla Greek yogurt, divided

½ cup sugar-free chocolate chips

½ cup raspberries

½ cup blueberries

¼ cup shredded unsweetened coconut

2 tablespoons creamy peanut butter, melted

Peel and slice bananas in half, and then in half again lengthwise.

Assemble banana splits by placing two banana sections on a plate or bowl. Top with ½ cup of yogurt. Garnish with chocolate chips, raspberries, blueberries, coconut, and melted peanut butter.

Per Serving: **Calories** 191 | **Fat** 4g | **Carb** 34g | **Fiber** 3g | **Sugar** 18g | **Protein** 8.5g

index

References to photographs are in *italic*.